A delighted Old Trafford crowd grab a glimpse of the league championship trophy in 1951/52

THE RACE FOR NO.19

Matt Busby and his players celebrate winning the 1956/57 championship with champagne in the dressing room bath

1956/57

THE RACE FOR NO.19

Denis Law leads out United followed by George Best, Nobby Stiles, Alex Stepney and John Aston as the team closed in on the 1966/67 league title

THE RACE FOR NO.19

2mania
Daily Mirror
MONDAY 18.05.2009
mirrorsport@mgn.co.uk

HOW THE TITLE WAS WON

HAPPY 18

Aug 17 United 1 Newcastle 1
Hardly a convincing start and it could have been worse after Obafemi Martins nodded the Toon in front. Darren Fletcher swiftly equalised but United could not find a winner.

Aug 25 Portsmouth 0 United 1
Fletcher again, with a scrambled deflected effort in the first half, but this time worth all three points as Ferguson's side avenged their FA Cup defeat over Pompey.

Sep 13 Liverpool 2 United 1
One to forget for United fans, despite Carlos Tevez's third-minute opener, with Nemanja Vidic sent off after Wes Brown's own goal and Ryan Babel notching the winner near the end. A game behind the rest but six points adrift of the pace.

Sep 21 Chelsea 1 United 1
A good point but one that left United 15th. Ji-Sung Park put them in front before Salomon Kalou scored the late leveller that put the Old Trafford side under pressure.

Sep 27 United 2 Bolton 0
The first contentious Old Trafford penalty of the season but not the last, as Ronaldo's blatant dive was rewarded with a spot-kick he himself converted before Wayne Rooney sealed the points. Still, however, in the bottom half.

Oct 4 Blackburn 0 United 2
Not for long and the win at Ewood increased the pressure on the struggling Paul Ince. Brown headed United in front as Vidic blocked off the keeper before Rooney converted Ronaldo's low cross.

Oct 18 United 4 West Brom 0
Now back in the groove and the promoted Baggies were no match for them once Rooney broke the deadlock before the hour. Ronaldo made it two before Dimitar Berbatov broke his league duck, Nani twisting the knife.

Oct 25 Everton 1 United 1
More points dropped after Fletcher put the champions ahead. Marouane Fellaini levelled and former United striker Louis Saha was the thickness of the woodwork away from winning it for the Toffees.

Oct 29 United 2 West Ham 0
All over inside half an hour but while Ronaldo claimed the brace, Berbatov's beautiful footwork before setting up the second was the real highlight of a canter.

Nov 1 United 4 Hull 3
What looked like a mauling turned into a nervous finale. Michael Carrick and a Ronaldo double made it look comfortable especially when Vidic added a fourth before the hour, only for the Tigers to bite back and make it close.

Nov 8 Arsenal 2 United 1
Nobody saw this coming, especially not Fergie and certainly not after United dominated early on. But two from Samir Nasri changed everything despite Rafael Da Silva's terrific first goal for the club. Back down to fourth.

Nov 15 United 5 Stoke 0
The start of the record-breaking defensive run and Stoke were simply swamped. Ronaldo and Carrick scored before the break, Berbatov added another and Danny Welbeck and Ronaldo completed the rout late on.

Nov 22 Aston Villa 0 United 0
A bitterly cold evening saw plenty of chances at both ends but none taken, Rooney missing the best of them. The sight of Ferguson scrambling in the dirt to retrieve the ball in the last seconds summed up United's frustrations.

Nov 30 Man City 0 United 1
Money can buy you most things in football but not real quality and the derby win showed that even though Ronaldo was controversially red-carded by Howard Webb for a handling offence. Rooney's first half goal proved decisive.

Dec 6 United 1 Sunderland 0
One of the pivotal results. United smashed on the door all game but it wasn't going to happen, only for Vidic to follow up and ram home as Carrick's deflected shot during injury time hit the post.

Dec 13 Tottenham 0 United 0
Another away-day blank and one that might have got away as both sides had their opportunities. Not the ideal send-off for the FIFA Club World Cup but United landed in Tokyo to hear Chelsea had been held by West Ham the next day.

Dec 26 Stoke 0 United 1
More dropped points by Liv and Chelsea during their stay in the Far East were early Christmas presents and United helped themselves on Boxing Day when Carlos Tevez capitalised on Berbatov's approach work seven minutes from time against the 10-man Po

Dec 29 United 1 M'brough 0
A seventh clean sheet meant three points as Boro's plunge towards the began in earnest. Berbatov scor only goal midway through the s half to keep Liverpool within ran

CHAMPS
United celebrate with the Premier League trophy after their goalless draw against Arsenal

R UNITED.. GAME BY GAME ...TH, SIR ALEX

mania 3
Daily Mirror
MONDAY 18.05.2009
mirrorsport@mgn.co.uk

Jan 11 United 3 Chelsea 0
This was even more emphatic than the scoreline suggests with Chelsea utterly outclassed as the Scolari reign lurched into crisis. Vidic nodded the opener and second-half strikes from Rooney and Berbatov emphasised the quality gap.

Jan 14 United 1 Wigan 0
Rooney scored from United's first attack in the opening minute and that proved enough as they moved up into second. Wigan huffed and puffed but have still to earn a single point against Fergie's men.

Jan 17 Bolton 0 United 1
Better late than never, they say, and Berbatov's injury-time intervention was another massive blow in the race for the crown as it took United top for the first time all season. Liverpool's draw with Everton two days later keeping them there.

Jan 27 West Brom 0 United 5
Compelling and comprehensive even before Paul Robinson was dismissed. Berbatov and Tevez – after a Scott Carson howler – put United on control before the break and after Vidic headed home Ronaldo waltzed in for two more.

Jan 31 United 1 Everton 0
Everton's resistance was broken when Mikel Arteta was adjudged to have fouled Carrick – even Fergie said there was no intent – but Ronaldo picked his spot to extend United's advantage over Liverpool to five points.

Feb 8 West Ham 0 United 1
United had lost on their previous two visits to Upton Park but it was third time lucky courtesy of Ryan Giggs' mazy run from the left and fine low finish, continuing his remarkable record of scoring in every Premier League season.

Feb 18 United 3 Fulham 0
Becoming ludicrously easy, helped by Fulham's supine display, Paul Scholes, Berbatov and Rooney all finding the net as Old Trafford prepared to crown their heroes long before the end of the season.

Feb 21 United 2 Blackburn 1
United's remarkable run had to end but it was perhaps inevitable that Edwin van der Sar was not the keeper to be beaten after 1,334 minutes when Roque Santa Cruz beat Thomas Kuszczak to level after Rooney's opener. Ronaldo, inevitably, scored the magnificent free-kick winner.

Mar 5 Newcastle 1 United 2
More defensive vulnerability, van der Sar culpable as Peter Lovenkrands put Newcastle in front. Rooney equalised and poor defending at the other end saw Berbatov pop home the goal that counted for the 11th straight win.

Mar 14 United 1 Liverpool 4
Another win would have sealed it but Liverpool had different ideas, despite trailing to Ronaldo's early penalty. Fernando Torres punished Vidic to level. Steven Gerrard scored from the spot and when Vidic was dismissed for fouling the England ace, Fabio Aurelio and Andrea Dossena rubbed it in.

Mar 21 Fulham 2 United 0
A wobble? Or maybe a full-blown crisis. United were simply awful, second best all game and trailing from Danny Murphy's early penalty which saw Scholes dismissed. Ronaldo's petulance helped Rooney see red as well, with Zoltan Gera sealing it. Pressure on.

Apr 5 United 3 Aston Villa 2
Crisis time – and time for a hero. Few United fans had even heard of Federico Macheda but his injury-time exploits, after Villa had led with 10 minutes to go, were the stuff of legend, even overshadowing Ronaldo's double.

Apr 11 Sunderland 1 United 2
Macheda again and this time within seconds of coming off the bench. United had been made to struggle, with Kenwyne Jones equalising Scholes' rare headed opener but Macheda's first touch diverted home and while Liverpool kept on winning, so did Fergie's men.

Apr 22 United 2 Portsmouth 0
Liverpool's incredible 4-4 draw with Arsenal took the pressure off and United eased home. Rooney put them on their way before Carrick strode through eight minutes from time. In their hands now.

Apr 25 United 5 Tottenham 2
And at half-time, almost out of them as Spurs led through Darren Bent and Luka Modric. Enter ref Howard Webb, seeing the foul on Carrick that nobody else did, and once Ronaldo stroked home the floodgates opened. Rooney adding two either side of another from Ronaldo before Berba finished it off.

May 2 Middlesbrough 0 United 2
Fergie rested most of his first team ahead of the second leg against Arsenal but this was no contest once Giggs picked his spot from 25 yards. Park grabbed the second soon after the break and it was cruise control.

May 11 United 2 Man City 0
Liverpool were not letting up but United, knowing they could win it before their rivals played again, would not give them a glimmer. This was too easy, with Ronaldo's strop after being subbed more entertaining than the game. The Portugal star and Tevez – a rebuke to Ferguson – did the business.

May 13 Wigan 1 United 2
Tougher this time, with Wigan in front at the break through Hugo Rodallega. But Tevez flicked home within three minutes of coming off the bench and Carrick's left-footer completed the comeback. One point needed.

May 16 United 0 Arsenal 0
One point required, one point earned and hardly a vintage show. Not that anybody really cared. Mission accomplished. Champions. Again.

09

ANTS
OOL 1
1977
F.A. CUP
FINAL
Official
Souvenir
EUROPEAN CUP
HE DATE...
ALEX
EPNEY
ALEX STEPNEY
THERE'S
ONLY ONE
UNITED
GEOFFREY GREEN
THE
OFFICIAL
CENTENARY
HISTORY OF
MANCHESTER
UNITED
1878
1978

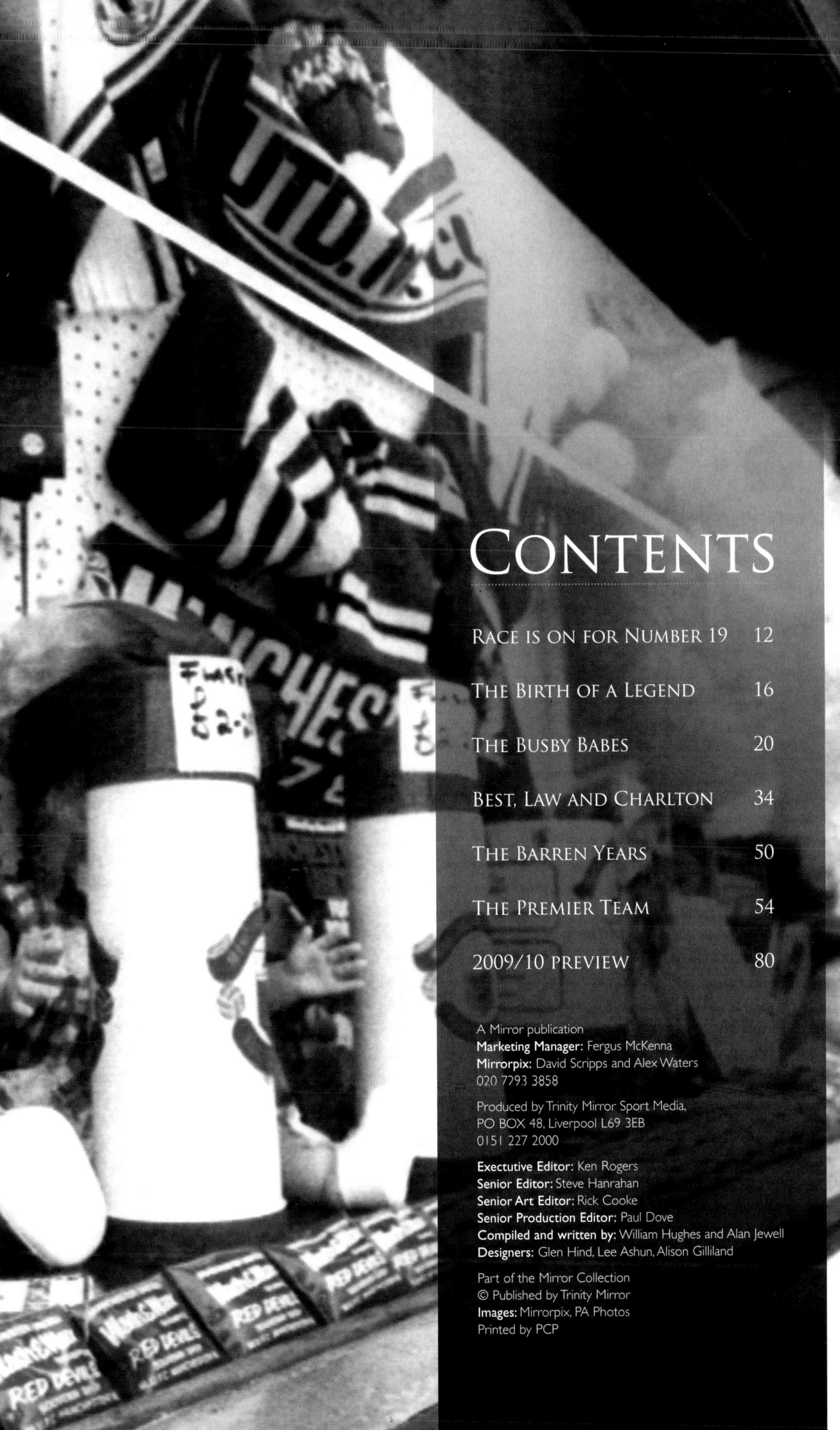

Contents

Race is on for Number 19   12

The Birth of a Legend   16

The Busby Babes   20

Best, Law and Charlton   34

The Barren Years   50

The Premier Team   54

2009/10 preview   80

A Mirror publication
Marketing Manager: Fergus McKenna
Mirrorpix: David Scripps and Alex Waters
020 7293 3858

Produced by Trinity Mirror Sport Media,
PO BOX 48, Liverpool L69 3EB
0151 227 2000

Exectutive Editor: Ken Rogers
Senior Editor: Steve Hanrahan
Senior Art Editor: Rick Cooke
Senior Production Editor: Paul Dove
Compiled and written by: William Hughes and Alan Jewell
Designers: Glen Hind, Lee Ashun, Alison Gilliland

Part of the Mirror Collection
© Published by Trinity Mirror
Images: Mirrorpix, PA Photos
Printed by PCP

Race is on for Number 19

MANCHESTER AND LIVERPOOL. TWO CITIES IN THE NORTH-WEST OF ENGLAND; ONE OF THE BIGGEST RIVALRIES IN WORLD FOOTBALL. THE CLUBS FROM THE RED HALVES OF THEIR RESPECTIVE HOMES NOW HAVE 18 TITLES APIECE. WHO WILL GET TO 19 FIRST?

DESPITE Manchester United's overwhelming dominance since the inception of the Premier League in 1992, Liverpool supporters have always been able to throw the weight of their history back at United followers.

No longer. The two most famous clubs in English football now stand level on 18 league championships and the general consensus is that one of them will end 2009/10 with 19.

A thrilling nine month-campaign lies ahead as United aim to overtake Liverpool's title tally for the first time while Rafael Benitez's team attempt to end their club's 20-year wait for a championship.

The enmity that has developed between Benitez and Sir Alex Ferguson will only add spice to the contest. Expect plenty of references to 'mind games' in the season ahead.

The history the clubs can boast gives the rivalry an edge that is missing when United take on Chelsea, whose significant achievements are largely restricted to the 21st century.

It was at the start of the 20th century that Liverpool first registered a league title win, in 1900/01, and since then United have generally been playing catch-up.

After 1910/11 the score was 2-2 but as the 1950s dawned Liverpool had a 5-2 lead. Sir Matt Busby led United to three titles within six seasons in the 1950s to level the scores again but the tragedy of Munich prevented his Babes from going on to achieve more.

From 1963/64 the sides alternated championships for four seasons and the tally remained at 7-7 until Liverpool triumphed in 1972/73.

This was the beginning of a spell where Liverpool reigned supreme, winning 11 titles within 18 seasons.

During this period United strove unsuccessfully to claim just one championship, a drought that became a saga in itself. At the start of every season the question would be posed: Will this be the year? United would always be found wanting and the embarrassment was exacerbated by what the team at the other end of the East Lancashire Road was achieving.

As their run ended in 1990, so United came to the fore. After a near miss in 1992, they finally claimed the championship in 1993. This was the first of 11 titles in 17 seasons, a ratio slightly better than Liverpool managed from 1973-1990.

This magazine celebrates all 18 of Manchester United's championship wins and the players who made them possible, together with the

Best and Law: Remembering one of the game's all-time greats, left. Above: Denis Law displays the league championship trophy in 1965

SETTING THE SCENE

Passions running high: Tempers flare during the clash between United and Arsenal at Old Trafford in October 1990 as referee Keith Hackett tries to intervene. United were docked a point for their part in the brawl, Arsenal two

United legend: Sir Matt Busby relaxing in his office at Old Trafford after leading United to the 1967 league title

legendary managers Sir Matt Busby and Sir Alex Ferguson, who have masterminded 16 of them.

There are a series of memorable and rarely seen Daily Mirror images featuring great names such as Billy Meredith, the Welsh wizard who starred in United's first two title-winning sides.

Into the 1950s and there is the poignancy of looking at the youthful innocence of the Busby Babes; young men of brilliance like Duncan Edwards, Tommy Taylor and Roger Byrne, who were so cruelly taken from us at Munich.

The 1960s brought us Best, Law and Charlton, superstars who were among the first footballers to transcend the sport.

Bryan Robson carried the fight during the barren years and was still around when championships started to be won again, as the likes of Eric Cantona, Peter Schmeichel, Mark Hughes and Ryan Giggs established themselves as United icons.

They were to be joined by serial winners of recent seasons who include Rio Ferdinand, Nemanja Vidic, Cristiano Ronaldo and Wayne Rooney.

We reproduce reports from the pages of the Mirror as they appeared at the time, which document every one of the 18 title wins and bring the achievements to life.

There are two constants from championships one and 11 in United's Premier League run: Ferguson and Giggs, two men whose desire has not been dimmed by the advancing years. With neat symmetry Giggs was PFA Young Player of the Year in 1992/93 and PFA Player of the Year in 2008/09.

How both would love to make it a round dozen in 2009/10 and give Manchester United a league title lead over Liverpool for the first time in history.

Let battle commence.

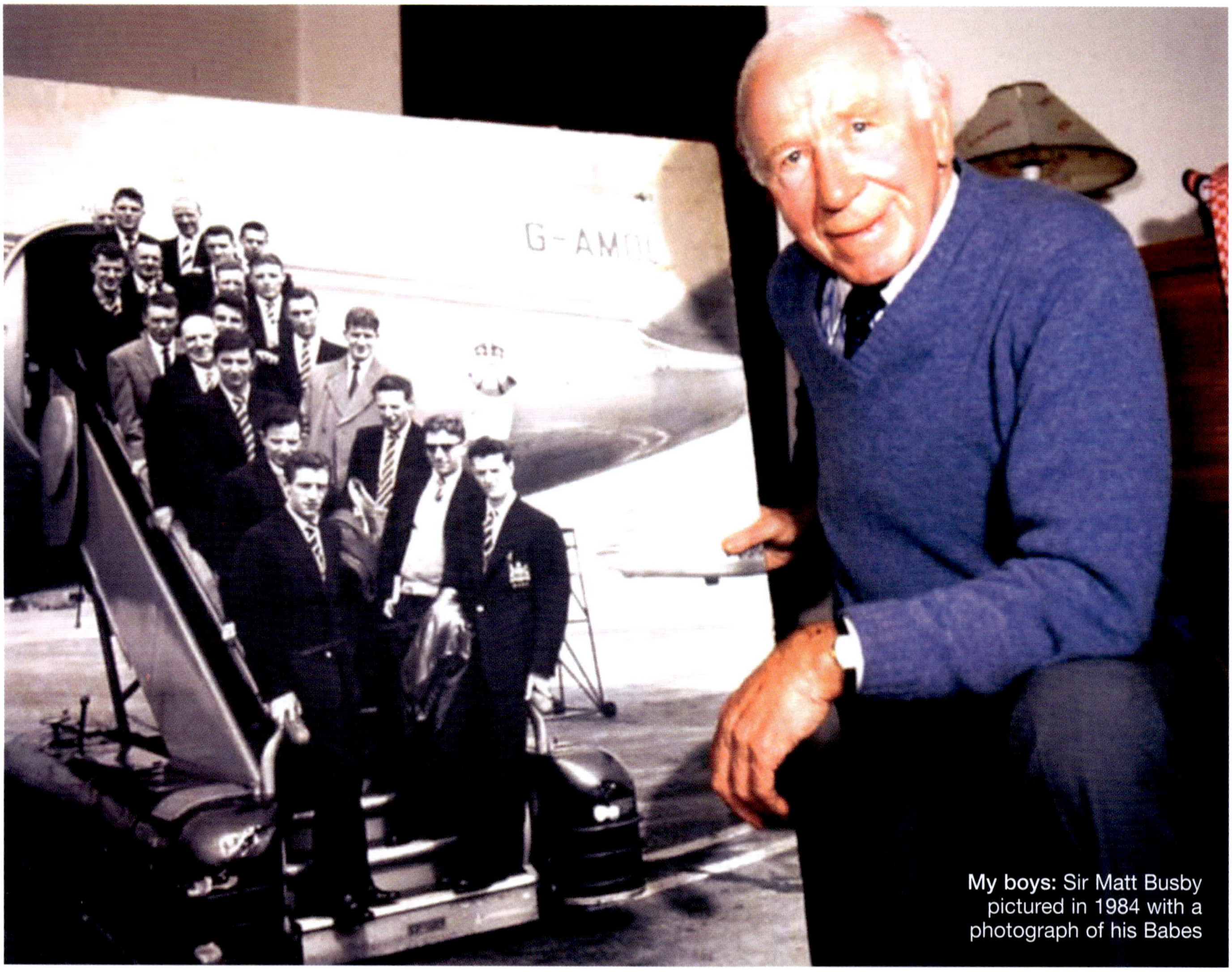

THE RACE FOR NO.19

My boys: Sir Matt Busby pictured in 1984 with a photograph of his Babes

Loyal supporters: Fans brave the elements to salute their heroes after United's FA Cup win in 1983

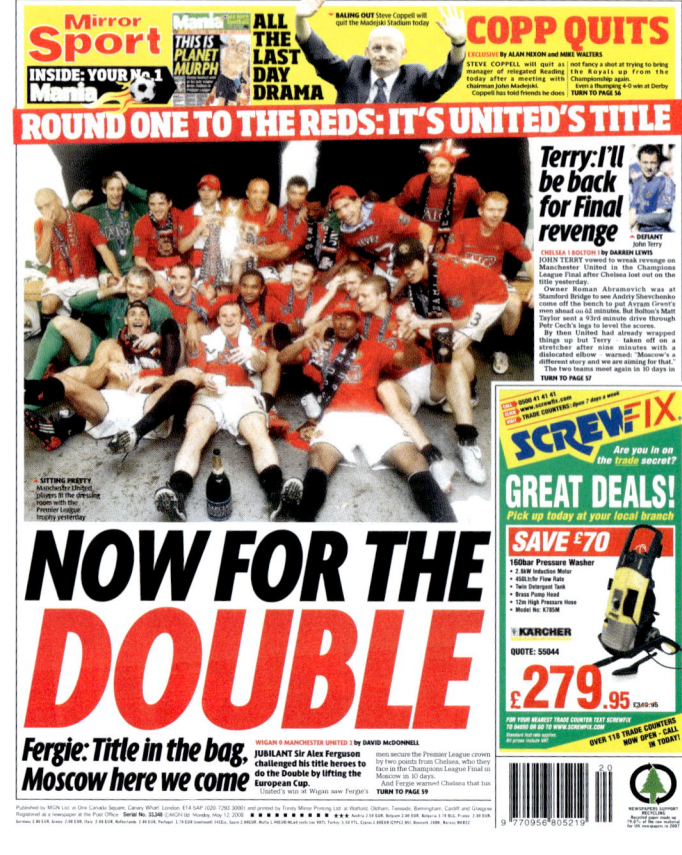

Right: How the Daily Mirror reported the Premier League title win of 2007/08, ahead of the Champions League final against Chelsea

SETTING THE SCENE

Bridging the divide: Phil Chisnall played for both United and Liverpool in the 1960s

Behind the wheel: Denis Law in his red Jaguar in July 1964

Bobby dazzler: Bobby Charlton in full flight during the 1960s

MANCHESTER UNITED V LIVERPOOL DECADE BY DECADE

1900-1910
1900/01:	Liverpool league champions
1905/06:	Liverpool league champions
1907/08:	Manchester United league champions
1908:	Manchester United Charity Shield winners
1908/09:	Manchester United FA Cup winners

1910-1920
1910/11:	Manchester United league champions
1911:	Manchester United Charity Shield winners

1910-1920
1921/22:	Liverpool league champions
1922/23:	Liverpool league champions

1930-1940
No major trophies won by either side

1940-1950
1946/47:	Liverpool league champions
1947/48:	Manchester United FA Cup winners

1950-1960
1951/52:	Manchester United league champions
1952:	Manchester United Charity Shield winners
1955/56:	Manchester United league champions
1956:	Manchester United Charity Shield winners
1956/57:	Manchester United league champions
1957:	Manchester United Charity Shield winners

1960-1970
1962/63:	Manchester United FA Cup winners
1963/64:	Liverpool league champions
1964:	Liverpool Charity Shield shared
1964/65:	Manchester United league champions
	Liverpool FA Cup winners
1965:	Manchester United and Liverpool share Charity Shield
1965/66:	Liverpool league champions
1966:	Liverpool Charity Shield winners
1966/67:	Manchester United league champions
1967:	Manchester United Charity Shield shared
1967/68:	Manchester United European Cup winners

1970-1980
1972/73:	Liverpool league champions
	Liverpool UEFA Cup winners
1973/74:	Liverpool FA Cup winners
1974:	Liverpool Charity Shield winners
1975/76:	Liverpool league champions
	Liverpool UEFA Cup winners
1976:	Liverpool Charity Shield winners
1976/77:	Liverpool league champions
	Liverpool European Cup winners
	Manchester United FA Cup winners
1977:	Manchester United and Liverpool share Charity Shield
1977/78:	Liverpool European Cup winners
	Liverpool European Super Cup winners
1978/79:	Liverpool league champions
1979:	Liverpool Charity Shield winners
1979/80:	Liverpool league champions

1980-1990
1980:	Liverpool Charity Shield winners
1980/81:	Liverpool European Cup winners
	Liverpool League Cup winners
1981/82:	Liverpool league champions
	Liverpool League Cup winners
1982:	Liverpool Charity Shield winners
1982/83:	Liverpool league champions
	Manchester United FA Cup winners
	Liverpool League Cup winners
1983:	Manchester United Charity Shield winners
1983/84:	Liverpool league champions
	Liverpool European Cup winners
	Liverpool League Cup winners
1984/85:	Manchester United FA Cup winners
1985/86:	Liverpool league champions
	Liverpool FA Cup winners
1986:	Liverpool Charity Shield shared
1987/88:	Liverpool league champions
1988:	Liverpool Charity Shield winners
1988/89:	Liverpool FA Cup winners
1989:	Liverpool Charity Shield winners
1989/90:	Liverpool league champions
	Manchester United FA Cup winners

1990-2000
1990:	Manchester United and Liverpool share Charity Shield
1990/91:	Manchester United European Cup Winners' Cup winners
1991/92:	Liverpool FA Cup winners
	Manchester United League Cup winners
	Manchester United European Super Cup winners
1992/93:	Manchester United league champions
1993:	Manchester United Charity Shield winners
1993/94:	Manchester United league champions
	Manchester United FA Cup winners
1994:	Manchester United Charity Shield winners
1994/95:	Liverpool League Cup winners
1995/96:	Manchester United league champions
	Manchester United FA Cup winners
1996:	Manchester United Charity Shield winners
1996/97:	Manchester United league champions
1997:	Manchester United Charity Shield winners
1998/99:	Manchester United league champions
	Manchester United European Cup winners
	Manchester United FA Cup winners
1999/00:	Manchester United league champions
	Manchester United Intercontinental Cup winners

2000-2009
2000/01:	Manchester United league champions
	Liverpool UEFA Cup winners
	Liverpool FA Cup winners
	Liverpool League Cup winners
2001:	Liverpool Charity Shield winners
2001/02:	Liverpool European Super Cup winners
2002/03:	Manchester United league champions
	Liverpool League Cup winners
2003:	Manchester United Community Shield winners
2003/04:	Manchester United FA Cup winners
2004/05:	Liverpool European Cup winners
2005/06:	Liverpool European Super Cup winners
	Manchester United League Cup winners
2006:	Liverpool Community Shield winners
2006/07:	Manchester United league champions
2007:	Manchester United Community Shield winners
2007/08:	Manchester United league champions
	Manchester United European Cup winners
2008:	Manchester United Community Shield winners
2008/09:	Manchester United league champions
	Manchester United Club World Championship winners

THE BIRTH OF A LEGEND

UNITED'S ROAD TO GLORY KICKED OFF IN THE EARLY 1900S. ORIGINALLY FORMED AS NEWTON HEATH, THE CLUB WERE RE-NAMED MANCHESTER UNITED IN 1902 AND SIX YEARS LATER THEY CLAIMED THEIR FIRST LEAGUE TITLE. IT WOULD BE THE FIRST OF MANY

Welsh wizard: Billy Meredith pictured circa 1908 with cups, caps and medals including the league championship

MEREDITH INSPIRES EARLY SUCCESSES

PROMOTED to the First Division in 1905/06, United consolidated in their first top-flight season as they finished eighth.

The events of the previous summer would help them in their quest for a first league title. Rivals Manchester City had been under investigation for paying some of their players a salary over the amount allowed by FA regulations. City were fined £250 and 18 of their players were banned from playing for them again. United swooped to snap up several of their players, including the Welsh wizard Billy Meredith and Sandy Turnbull. The new boys from across town were ineligible to play until New Year's Day 1907, due to their suspension, so it was the 1907/08 season before they could make a proper impact on United's bid for the title.

They did just that with a run of 10 consecutive victories and despite a shaky end to the season, United hung on to claim their first title, ending the campaign nine points ahead of runners-up Aston Villa.

1909 saw United win their first FA Cup with Turnbull scoring the winning goal in the final and in February 1910 the club moved to a new home at Old Trafford.

The first full season at their new headquarters, 1910/11, saw United crowned champions for the second season. As United fans enjoyed the taste of victory, they were not to know it would be the last time their club would win the First Division for another 41 years, the longest spell in their history they have gone without winning the top-flight.

FINAL TABLE 1907/08

		Pld	W	D	L	F	A	GA	Pts
1	Manchester United	38	23	6	9	81	48	1.69	52
2	Aston Villa	38	17	9	12	77	59	1.30	43
3	Manchester City	38	16	11	11	62	54	1.15	43
4	Newcastle United	38	15	12	11	65	54	1.20	42
5	Sheffield Wednesday	38	19	4	15	73	64	1.14	42
6	Middlesbrough	38	17	7	14	54	45	1.20	41
7	Bury	38	14	11	13	58	61	0.95	39
8	Liverpool	38	16	6	16	68	61	1.11	38
9	Nottingham Forest	38	13	11	14	59	62	0.95	37
10	Bristol City	38	12	12	14	58	61	0.95	36
11	Everton	38	15	6	17	58	64	0.91	36
12	Preston North End	38	12	12	14	47	53	0.89	36
13	Chelsea	38	14	8	16	53	62	0.86	36
14	Arsenal	38	12	12	14	51	63	0.81	36
15	Blackburn Rovers	38	12	12	14	51	63	0.81	36
16	Sunderland	38	16	3	19	78	75	1.04	35
17	Sheffield United	38	12	11	15	52	58	0.90	35
18	Notts County	38	13	8	17	39	51	0.77	34
19	Bolton Wanderers	38	14	5	19	52	58	0.90	33
20	Birmingham City	38	9	12	17	40	60	0.67	30

THE DAILY MIRROR.

LEAGUES IN THEIR FINAL STAGES.

Manchester U. and Q. P. Rangers Certain Champions.

IMPORTANT GAMES IN DIVISION II.

The end of the football season is rapidly approaching, and after to-day only two Saturdays are left for league matches, although, of course, a few games will be played after April 25 and before the day dreaded by footballers, May 1.

Manchester United, who will be champions of the First Division, indisputably deserve the reward they are to have. Although during the last month they have not shown the fine form they displayed earlier in the season, they are a brilliant combination, and a team, had they had a little more luck, quite capable of winning the League championship and the F.A. Cup.

However, it is perhaps as well the honours should be distributed, and the future champions are quite content with their season's work. Since the end of September their position at the head of the table has never been seriously challenged, and there is rather more interest now in speculating on the team to be the runners-up. This distinction may fall to Sheffield Wednesday or Manchester City, although four or five clubs are in the running, as will be seen from the following positions:—

	Plyd.	Won	Lost	Drwn.	For	Agst.	Pts.
Manchester United	32	23	6	4	76	40	48
Sheffield Wednesday	33	18	13	2	68	56	38
Manchester City	33	15	10	8	69	50	38
Newcastle United	34	13	9	12	58	47	38
Middlesbrough	35	15	13	7	51	43	37
Aston Villa	33	13	11	9	69	54	35

Newsflash: The Daily Mirror reports on United's impending first title in 1908. On the far right of the opposite page, the Mirror previews the final day of the 1910/11 season and, below that, describes how Aston Villa were leapfrogged as United were crowned champions for a second time

THE BIRTH OF A LEGEND

In training: Billy Meredith at work in 1915

FINAL TABLE 1910/11

		Pld	W	D	L	F	A	GA	Pts
1	Manchester United	38	22	8	8	72	40	1.80	52
2	Aston Villa	38	22	7	9	69	41	1.68	51
3	Sunderland	38	15	15	8	67	48	1.40	45
4	Everton	38	19	7	12	50	36	1.39	45
5	Bradford City	38	20	5	13	51	42	1.21	45
6	Sheffield Wednesday	38	17	8	13	47	48	0.98	42
7	Oldham Athletic	38	16	9	13	44	41	1.07	41
8	Newcastle United	38	15	10	13	61	43	1.42	40
9	Sheffield United	38	15	8	15	49	43	1.14	38
10	Arsenal	38	13	12	13	41	49	0.84	38
11	Notts County	38	14	10	14	37	45	0.82	38
12	Blackburn Rovers	38	13	11	14	62	54	1.15	37
13	Liverpool	38	15	7	16	53	53	1.00	37
14	Preston North End	38	12	11	15	40	49	0.82	35
15	Tottenham Hotspur	38	13	6	19	52	63	0.83	32
16	Middlesbrough	38	11	10	17	49	63	0.78	32
17	Manchester City	38	9	13	16	43	58	0.74	31
18	Bury	38	9	11	18	43	71	0.61	29
19	Bristol City	38	11	5	22	43	66	0.65	27
20	Nottingham Forest	38	9	7	22	55	75	0.73	25

THE DAILY MIRROR

LAST DAY OF THE FOOTBALL SEASON.

Matches Which Concern Promotion, Relegation and Championships.

CHELSEA'S FORLORN HOPE.

To-day ends the football season, and after the last few weeks of Cup-finals and League excitements we are all heartily glad. Where a football is being kicked a crowd will gather to see it. After to-day they will have to wait until next August, when the practice games come round. And King Cricket will hold sway during the summer months.

Chief interest in the remaining matches centres in the doings of the three clubs struggling for promotion; whether Aston Villa will retain the League championship or hand it over to Manchester United; and whether Bury or Bristol City is to accompany Nottingham Forest into the Second League, and nothing is settled.

Aston Villa have to visit Liverpool, and if they win there then they retain the honours they won last year. If they draw, they will probably win on goal average, unless the United trounce Sunderland badly at Manchester. As Sunderland have been enjoying a tour in Scotland this week, that is quite possible. Still, the Villa are playing so well now that I think they are pretty sure to beat Liverpool, and then Manchester might win by 10 to 0 and it would not avail them.

At the other end of the table the matches that are of moment are Bristol City v. Everton at Bristol, and Bury v. Sheffield United at Bury. If Bury win, then they save themselves from figuring in the Second Division next year. If they draw and Bristol beat Everton, then Bristol save themselves on goal average.

It is not a little curious that both the Liverpool clubs should be taking such a big hand in the important last-day matches. Bristol have been playing well lately, and are quite likely to beat Everton, but Bury, desperate for their position, are quite as likely to defeat Sheffield, and so the South looks like losing one of its representatives in the senior competition. The positions of the clubs and their records are appended:—

	Plyd.	Won.	Lost.	Drw.	For	Agst.	Pts.
1—Aston Villa	37	22	8	7	68	38	51
2—Manchester Utd.	37	21	8	8	67	39	50
18—Bury	37	9	18	10	42	70	28
19—Bristol City	37	11	21	5	43	65	27
20—Nottingham F.	38	9	22	7	55	75	25

THE DAILY MIRROR

WIND UP OF THE FOOTBALL SEASON.

Manchester United and West Bromwich Albion English League Champions.

CHELSEA AND BRISTOL FAIL.

The football season ended on Saturday, and all the hopes and aspirations of eight long winter months were set at rest. Successful clubs are looking forward to next winter with equanimity, and those who went through a bad time will be setting about the work of strengthening their teams for another campaign.

Chelsea, who all through the season were expected to regain their lost place in the First League, failed ignominiously at Gainsborough. Had they won they would have gone up on goal average, for Bolton were also beaten at Birmingham. This is bad luck for London and the South, but it would have been equally unfortunate for Bolton after leading the field for the greater part of the season.

West Bromwich Albion, a club which has been struggling for years to regain their place in the senior ranks, finished up champions and are to be heartily congratulated after the exasperating bad luck they have experienced during the last few seasons. They have been about the best and most consistent side in the Second League for some years, and I expect them to do well in the best company.

Aston Villa were beaten at Liverpool, and so Manchester United, who defeated Sunderland, wrest the championship from the Birmingham cracks. Bristol City were beaten at home by Everton; had they won they would have remained in the First League instead of Bury, by virtue of a better goal average. So Bristol and Nottingham Forest will play in the Second Division next year and the South will only have Tottenham Hotspur and Woolwich Arsenal in the First League. A word of congratulation is due to the Arsenal for the splendid manner in which they have finished up the season, and their win at Nottingham against the County was a fitting climax to grand work since Christmas.

At the bottom of the Second League Barnsley and Lincoln City have to apply for re-election. With the prospect of about ten clubs putting up for election at the general meeting, Lincoln's prospects are not particularly bright. Gainsborough would have filled Barnsley's berth but for their fine victory over Chelsea. The club is one of the old clubs of the League, and as their exclusion would probably have caused their extinction, perhaps the defeat of Chelsea is a good thing. Barnsley are almost sure to retain their place. It is too soon after their appearance in a final tie for them to be outvoted.

Swindon had already won the Southern League Shield, so it only remains for me to congratulate Reading on regaining their place in the First Division by winning the championship of the junior section. Stoke finished second, and also enter the 'upper circle.' Portsmouth, one time champions, sink to the second class, and are accompanied by Southend United. Millwall just scrambling out of the last places. The full League tables for the season are appended:—

THE RACE FOR NO.19

Captain Jack: A packed Old Trafford watches United captain Jack Wilson shake hands with Birmingham City's Joe Wilson ahead of United's FA Cup fourth round win in 1928

Duncan's Devils: Scott Duncan, pictured left, managed United between 1932 and 1937 and helped them back into the top flight as they won the Second Divison title in 1935/36

THE BIRTH OF A LEGEND

Pre-war action: Jack Griffiths, a defender who played 173 games for United, clears his lines during a trial match at Old Trafford in August 1938

Mutch ado: Far left is George Mutch who scored 49 goals for United between 1934 and 1938. He joined Preston North End and scored the winning goal in the 1938 FA Cup final, the first time it was televised

Between the sticks: United keeper Tommy Breen in action in April 1939

THE RACE FOR NO.19

THE BUSBY BABES

THEY THRILLED THE COUNTRY, NEVER MIND MANCHESTER, THROUGH THE 1950S AS UNITED'S YOUNG TEAM DOMINATED DOMESTIC FOOTBALL AND BECAME THE FIRST ENGLISH CLUB TO COMPETE IN THE EUROPEAN CUP, BEFORE TRAGEDY STRUCK AT MUNICH

Above: Manchester City's Maine Road became the club's residence after Old Trafford was bombed during World War II. United's home did not reopen until August 1949. Below is an image from the first game at the rebuilt stadium – a 3-0 defeat of Bolton

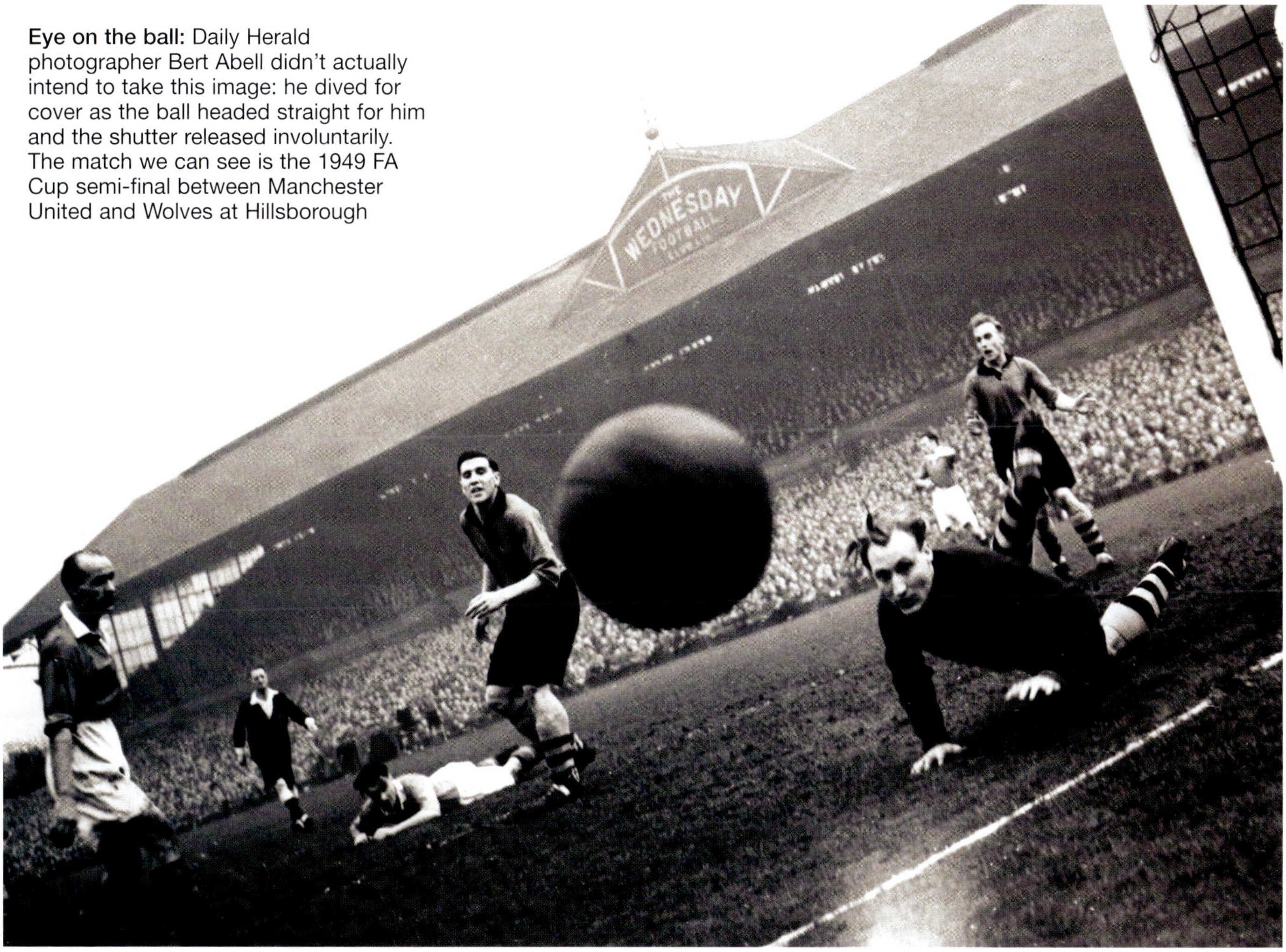

Eye on the ball: Daily Herald photographer Bert Abell didn't actually intend to take this image: he dived for cover as the ball headed straight for him and the shutter released involuntarily. The match we can see is the 1949 FA Cup semi-final between Manchester United and Wolves at Hillsborough

Daily Mirror TUES., APL. 15 FORWARD WITH THE PEOPLE

WORLD'S BIGGEST DAILY SALE

Last lap—neck and neck!

350,000 TRADE UNIONISTS DECIDE ON AN ALL-OUT WAGE WAR

By HAROLD HUTCHINSON

THE first of the big trade unions to meet since the Conservative Government was elected, yesterday adopted a series of resolutions which mean an all-out wage war.

The Government's policy for keeping the country solvent and saving the £ from a second devaluation involves trying to check any really big upward movement of wages.

The Government believes that, painful as it is at a time of rising prices, it is a lot less painful than the alternative which is continuing inflation and possible national bankruptcy.

But it was clear at the conference of the 350,000-strong union of Shop, Distributive and Allied Workers at Margate that its members will have none of this policy.

Mr. Alan Birch, general secretary of the union and a member of the General Council of the TUC, declared, amid the cheers of a thousand delegates, that in view of Mr. Butler's Budget "there can be no restraint in wages demands." "Obviously," he went on, "there can be no basis for moderation in wage demands when the Government abandons its responsibility to the people." By this he meant the cuts in food subsidies.

IT'S Manchester United and Arsenal all the way for this season's League championship.

United clobbered Burnley 6—1, Arsenal rolled over Blackpool by 4—1. United are two points ahead. Arsenal have an extra game to play.

With Portsmouth dumped out of the reckoning, beaten at Derby, and Spurs dropping a point at Preston, it looks like a two-way fight. And the climax? On Saturday week at Old Trafford, when the fixture lists will show "Manchester United v. Arsenal."

In the Second Division, the Sheffield-Birmingham see-saw goes on. Wednesday, with a 2—0 win, made it the holiday double over Brentford, and go to the top by a point.

A terrific 40yds. free kick goal from Alf Sherwood, Cardiff skipper, helped beat Birmingham 3—1 and put Cardiff back, if slightly, in the race.

Fulham went down again, at Bolton, and it looks as though Stoke, beaten by Charlton, are worrying, too. A great effort by Hull City in beating Everton gives them a ray of hope.

Crazy game by Queen's Park Rangers. They rapped on two against Sheffield United, saw United equalise in the second half, then in last seven minutes Rangers cracked in two more. Further joy for their fans—fifteen Cup Final tickets were balloted on programme numbers, by the supporters!

Unluckiest player in football? Laurie Hughes, Liverpool and England centre half. His first match since January lasted ten minutes. He was carried off with that same old knee injury.

RESULTS AND TABLES

DIVISION I

DIVISION II

DIVISION III (S.)

DIVISION III (N.)

Boro are safe —at last!

By FRANK McGHEE

FORGET the fact that Newcastle played minus five of their Cup side against Middlesbrough at Ayresome Park yesterday; ignore any ridiculous rumours that they were holding themselves back for Wembley. The plain truth is that Middlesbrough, who won 2—1, would have beaten any League side in the country on this showing.

They needed these two points to make absolutely certain of First Division football next season.

No wonder Blackpool's centre forward, Stephenson (white shirt), and Shaw, Arsenal centre half, nursed headaches after yesterday's match at Highbury. Joe Mercer, Arsenal captain, had a close-up of the collision. Arsenal won a match vital to their League championship hopes by four goals to one.

Rain ends match

Repair men warned of 'throw off' shoes

"Let's all go down the Strand"

MORE SOCCER ON PAGE 14

RACING ON PAGE 14

The Flutters

WEATHER

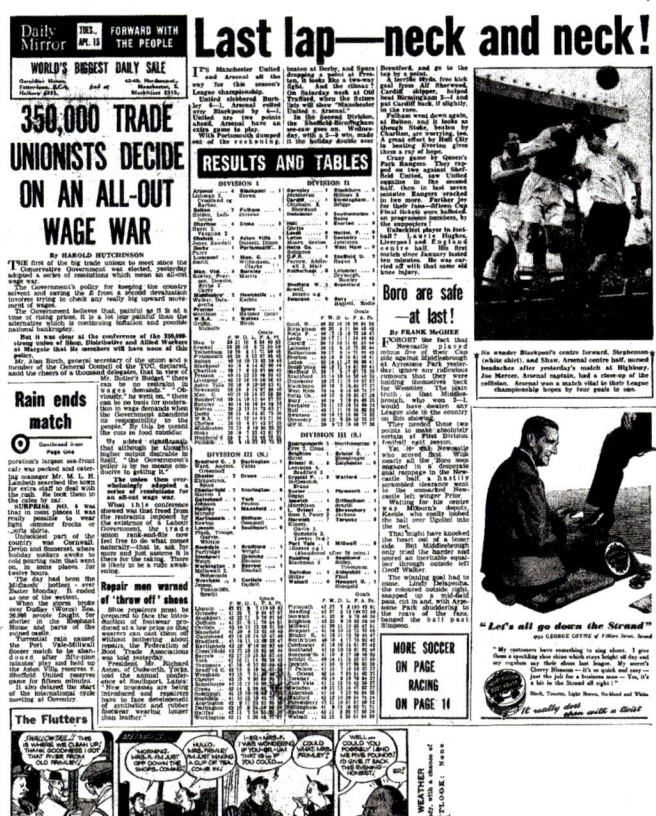

Race for the title: The Mirror's headline anticipates the final few games of the 1951/52 season, which saw United prevail over Spurs and Arsenal

FINAL TABLE 1951/52

		Pld	W	D	L	F	A	GA	Pts
1	Manchester United	42	23	11	8	95	52	1.83	57
2	Tottenham Hotspur	42	22	9	11	76	51	1.49	53
3	Arsenal	42	21	11	10	80	61	1.31	53
4	Portsmouth	42	20	8	14	68	58	1.17	48
5	Bolton Wanderers	42	19	10	13	65	61	1.07	48
6	Aston Villa	42	19	9	14	79	70	1.13	47
7	Preston North End	42	17	12	13	74	54	1.37	46
8	Newcastle United	42	18	9	15	98	73	1.34	45
9	Blackpool	42	18	9	15	64	64	1.00	45
10	Charlton Athletic	42	17	10	15	68	63	1.08	44
11	Liverpool	42	12	19	11	57	61	0.93	43
12	Sunderland	42	15	12	15	70	61	1.15	42
13	West Bromwich Albion	42	14	13	15	74	77	0.96	41
14	Burnley	42	15	10	17	56	63	0.89	40
15	Manchester City	42	13	13	16	58	61	0.95	39
16	Wolves	42	12	14	16	73	73	1.00	38
17	Derby County	42	15	7	20	63	80	0.79	37
18	Middlesbrough	42	15	6	21	64	88	0.73	36
19	Chelsea	42	14	8	20	52	72	0.72	36
20	Stoke City	42	12	7	23	49	88	0.56	31
21	Huddersfield Town	42	10	8	24	49	82	0.60	28
22	Fulham	42	8	11	23	58	77	0.75	27

THE RACE FOR NO.19

Well done, son: A handshake from assistant manager Jimmy Murphy for Duncan Edwards after he had made his first team debut in April 1953, aged 16. The main picture shows him training in August 1954

"If I shut my eyes I can see him now. Those pants hitched up, the wild leaps of boyish enthusiasm as he came running out of the tunnel. He played wing half, centre half, centre forward and inside forward with the consummate ease of a great player. He was quite simply a soccer colossus"

– Jimmy Murphy, former Manchester United assistant manager

THE RACE FOR NO.19

Tea for eleven: Manchester United players who lodged at Mrs Watson's Old Trafford guest house gather in September 1953. Clockwise from the bottom left (seated) are: Tommy Taylor, Mrs Watson, Bobby Charlton, Billy Whelan, Jackie Blanchflower, Mark Jones, Gordon Clayton, Alan Rhodes and Duncan Edwards. Right, Jackie Blanchflower has a go at the crossword in 1955, with Matt Busby on hand to offer some answers

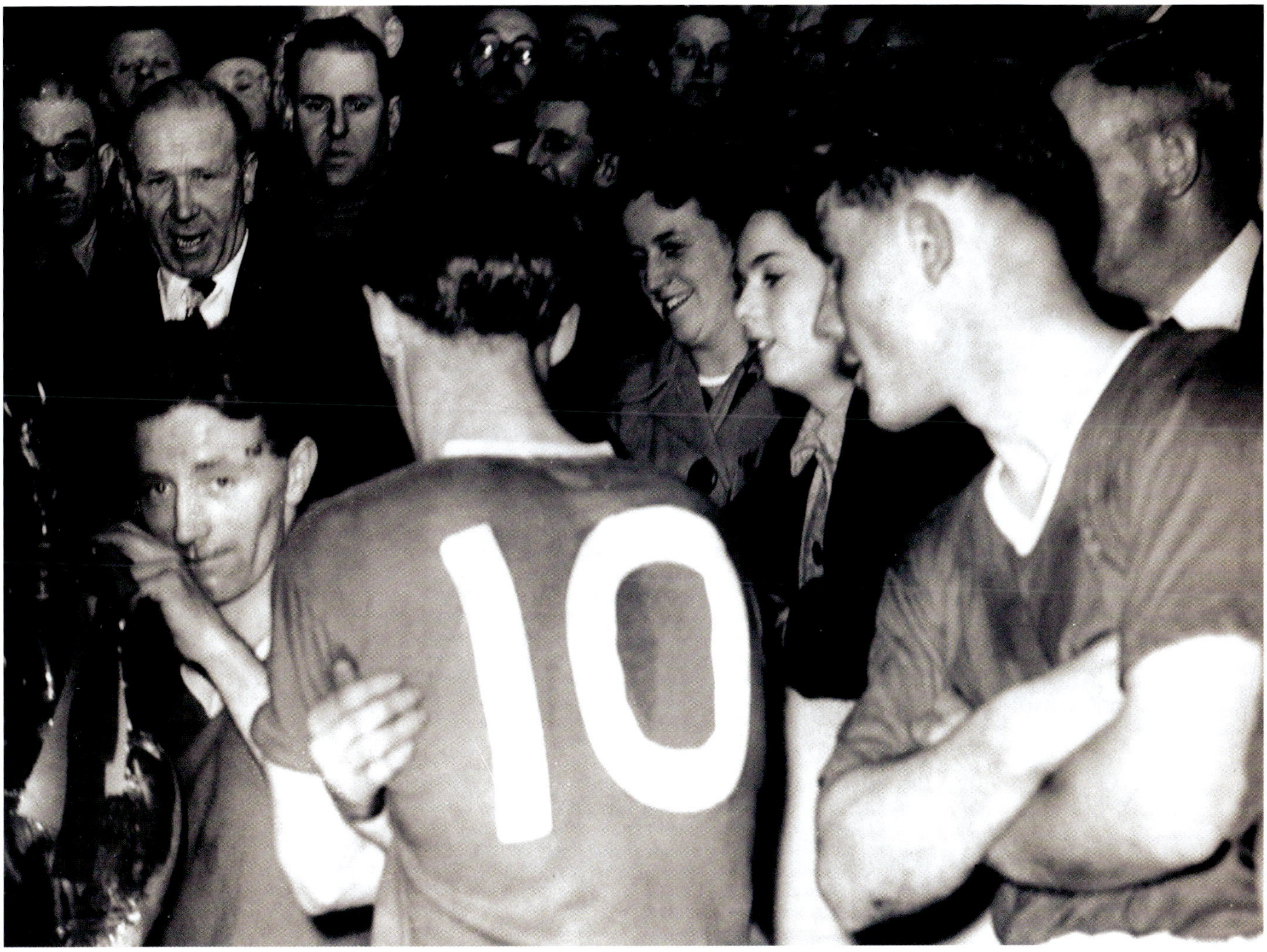

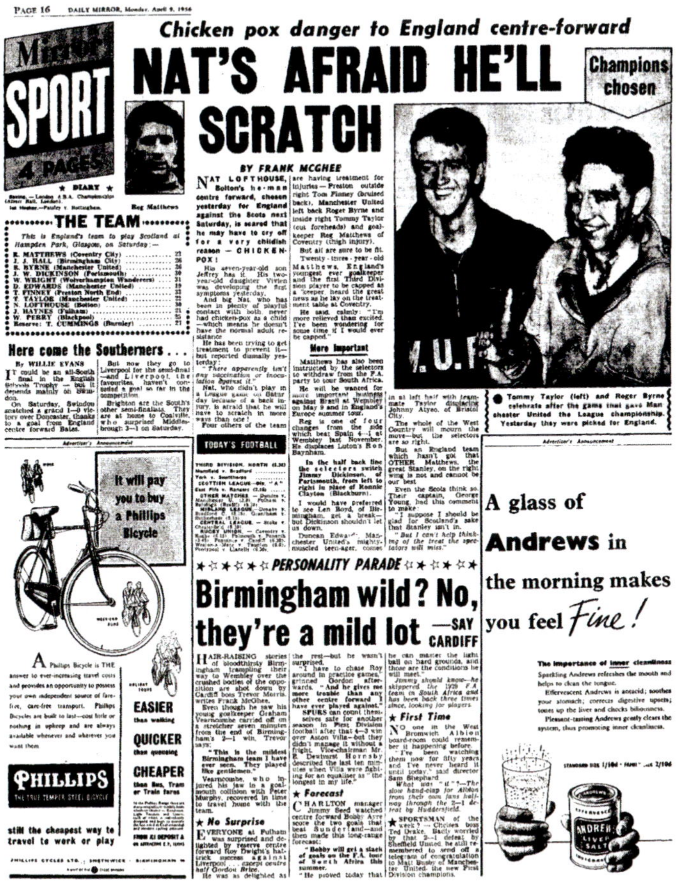

PAGE 16 DAILY MIRROR, Monday, April 9, 1956

Mirror SPORT 4 PAGES

Chicken pox danger to England centre-forward

NAT'S AFRAID HE'LL SCRATCH

Champions chosen

BY FRANK McGHEE

THE TEAM

Here come the Southerners . . .

Tommy Taylor (left) and Roger Byrne celebrate after the game that gave Manchester United the League championship. Yesterday they were picked for England.

TODAY'S FOOTBALL

PERSONALITY PARADE

Birmingham wild? No, they're a mild lot —SAY CARDIFF

It will pay you to buy a Phillips Bicycle

PHILLIPS

EASIER than walking

QUICKER than queueing

CHEAPER than Bus, Tram or Train fares

A glass of Andrews in the morning makes you feel Fine!

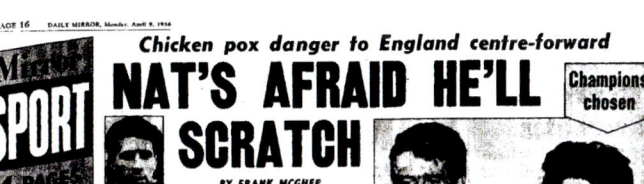

Above: Captain Roger Byrne, watched by Busby, with the championship trophy in April 1956. Left, Byrne and Tommy Taylor pictured in the Mirror after the title was clinched

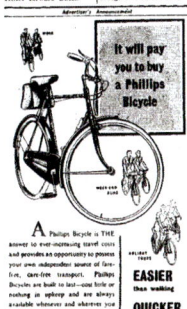

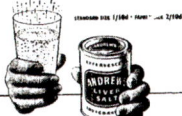

FINAL TABLE 1955/56

		Pld	W	D	L	F	A	GA	Pts
1	Manchester United	42	25	10	7	83	51	1.63	60
2	Blackpool	42	20	9	13	86	62	1.39	49
3	Wolves	42	20	9	13	89	65	1.37	49
4	Manchester City	42	18	10	14	82	69	1.19	46
5	Arsenal	42	18	10	14	60	61	0.98	46
6	Birmingham City	42	18	9	15	75	57	1.32	45
7	Burnley	42	18	8	16	64	54	1.19	44
8	Bolton Wanderers	42	18	7	17	71	58	1.22	43
9	Sunderland	42	17	9	16	80	95	0.84	43
10	Luton Town	42	17	8	17	66	64	1.03	42
11	Newcastle United	42	17	7	18	85	70	1.21	41
12	Portsmouth	42	16	9	17	78	85	0.92	41
13	West Bromwich Albion	42	18	5	19	58	70	0.83	41
14	Charlton Athletic	42	17	6	19	75	81	0.93	40
15	Everton	42	15	10	17	55	69	0.80	40
16	Chelsea	42	14	11	17	64	77	0.83	39
17	Cardiff City	42	15	9	18	55	69	0.80	39
18	Tottenham Hotspur	42	15	7	20	61	71	0.86	37
19	Preston North End	42	14	8	20	73	72	1.01	36
20	Aston Villa	42	11	13	18	52	69	0.75	35
21	Huddersfield Town	42	14	7	21	54	83	0.65	35
22	Sheffield United	42	12	9	21	63	77	0.82	33

Jump for joy: Johnny Berry, Duncan Edwards, Mark Jones, Roger Byrne and Dennis Viollet

Left: Byrne shows his strength in October 1956

Above: A big heave from Edwards, Berry, Viollet, Bill Foulkes, Byrne, Wilf McGuinness, Jones and Billy Whelan

THE BUSBY BABES

Jazz man: Tommy Taylor on saxaphone after United reached the FA Cup final in 1957. He is being watched by Billy Whelan and Wilf McGuinness

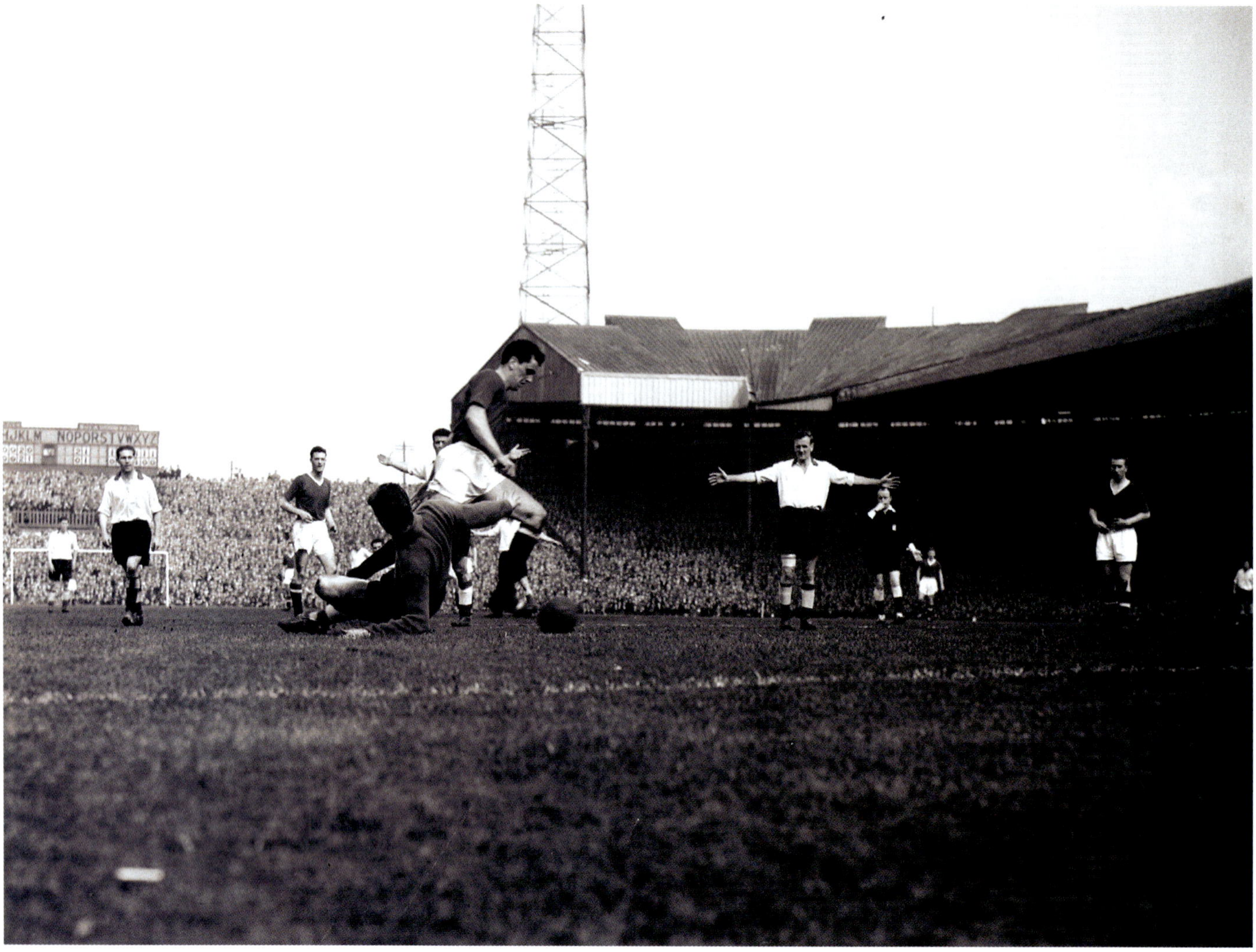

DAILY MIRROR, Monday, April 22, 1957

This is one to show the chaps

Champions feel strain of the fantastic treble

BABES EXHAUSTED—6 MAY MISS GAME TODAY

By FRANK McGHEE

FIXTURES AND 1-2-X CHECK

Decider

Awkward

FINNEY DOUBTFUL FOR WORLD CUP

DON'T BE AGGRESSIVE TO US PLEAD SPANIARDS

Davies can show what he has learned

'Something new' —and it brings Sheila a cap

Discovery

CROSSWORD

SPORTS SUMMARY

HOLIDAY DOG BETS

Saturday's Solution

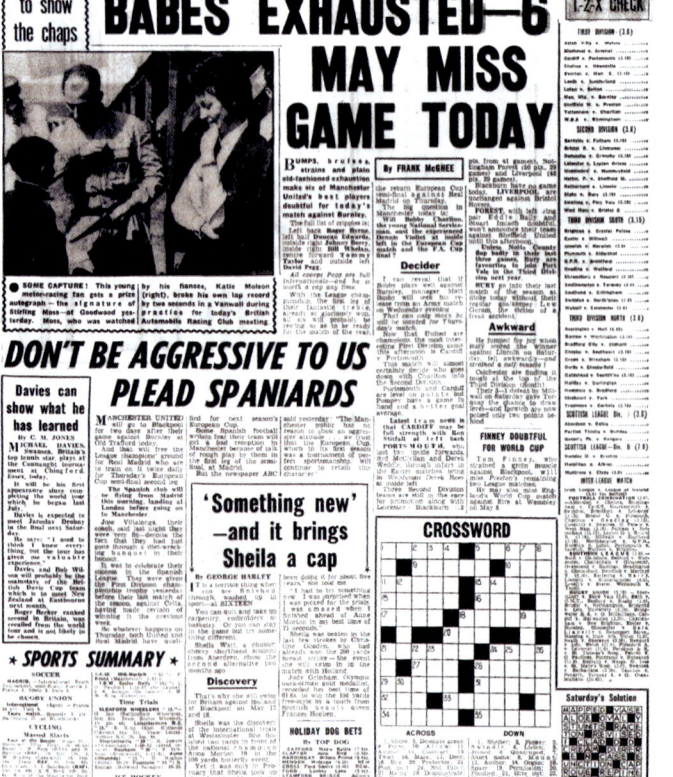

Above: United defeat Sunderland to clinch the championship in April 1957. The Mirror report, left, described how the team was feeling the strain of a hectic fixture list. They went on to lose in the European Cup semi-final and FA Cup final

FINAL TABLE 1956/57

		Pld	W	D	L	F	A	GA	Pts
1	Manchester United	42	28	8	6	103	54	1.91	64
2	Tottenham Hotspur	42	22	12	8	104	56	1.86	56
3	Preston North End	42	23	10	9	84	56	1.50	56
4	Blackpool	42	22	9	11	93	65	1.43	53
5	Arsenal	42	21	8	13	85	69	1.23	50
6	Wolves	42	20	8	14	94	70	1.34	48
7	Burnley	42	18	10	14	56	50	1.12	46
8	Leeds United	42	15	14	13	72	63	1.14	44
9	Bolton Wanderers	42	16	12	14	65	65	1.00	44
10	Aston Villa	42	14	15	13	65	55	1.18	43
11	West Bromwich Albion	42	14	14	14	59	61	0.97	42
12	Birmingham City	42	15	9	18	69	69	1.00	39
13	Chelsea	42	13	13	16	73	73	1.00	39
14	Sheffield Wednesday	42	16	6	20	82	88	0.93	38
15	Everton	42	14	10	18	61	79	0.77	38
16	Luton Town	42	14	9	19	58	76	0.76	37
17	Newcastle United	42	14	8	20	67	87	0.77	36
18	Manchester City	42	13	9	20	78	88	0.89	35
19	Portsmouth	42	10	13	19	62	92	0.67	33
20	Sunderland	42	12	8	22	67	88	0.76	32
21	Cardiff City	42	10	9	23	53	88	0.60	29
22	Charlton Athletic	42	9	4	29	62	120	0.52	22

THE BUSBY BABES

On your head, mum: Bobby Charlton competes in the street with his mother, Cissie

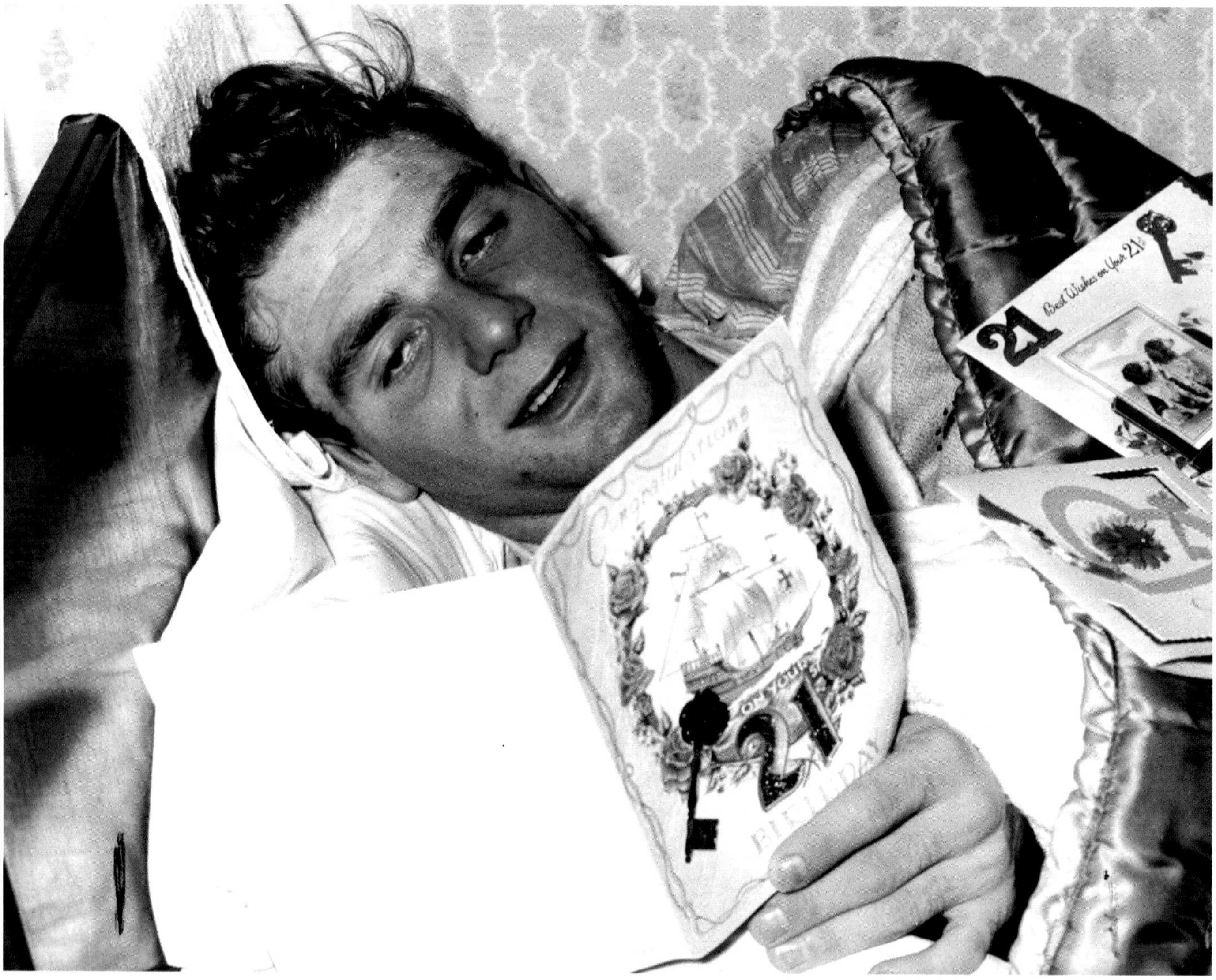

Above: Duncan Edwards in bed with 'flu on his 21st birthday in October 1957. He missed a European Cup tie against Shamrock Rovers

Right: A Manchester United team line-up in December 1957. Back row: Duncan Edwards, Bill Foulkes, Mark Jones, Ray Wood, Eddie Colman, David Pegg. Front row: Jimmy Berry, Billy Whelan, Roger Byrne, Tommy Taylor, Dennis Viollet

THE BUSBY BABES

Daily Mirror
FRI FEB 7 1958

2½ FORWARD WITH THE PEOPLE
No. 16,843

SOCCER AIR TRAGEDY
Manchester United plane crashes
22 dead

THE END The chartered Elizabethan airliner in which the Manchester United team was travelling home lies shattered in a snowfield near Munich. The pilot, Captain James Thain, escaped alive from the smashed nose (on the left of the picture).

THE BEGINNING This picture was taken when the team, accompanied by sports writers, boarded the plane at Manchester on Monday. Left to right, with known survivors marked with asterisk*: Jackie Blanchflower*; Billy Foulkes*; Walter Crickmer, secretary; Don Davies, Manchester Guardian; Roger Byrne, captain; Duncan Edwards*; Albert Scanlon*—just visible behind Scanlon is Frank Swift, News of the World; Ray Wood*; Denis Viollet*; Archie Ledbrooke, Daily Mirror; Geoff Bent; Mark Jones and Alf Clarke, Kemsley Newspapers.

AN Elizabethan airliner, on charter to the fabulous Manchester United football team, crashed in flames at Munich Airport, Germany, yesterday, and plunged the world of Soccer into mourning.

Last night twenty-two men—among them some of the brightest stars in British football—were feared to have died in the crash.

Seven of them were members of the champion Manchester United football team—such international stars as Roger Byrne, the team captain, and centre forward Tommy Taylor.

Twenty-two of the forty-four people aboard the plane survived, including Matt Busby, the team's famous manager, two air hostesses and a baby.

Among those who died was Archie Ledbrooke, the Mirror's famous Northern sports writer.

● THE CRASH—Story and pictures: Back Page.
● THE TEAM in the Tragedy—See Centre Pages.

─Blackest Day of─
All—By Peter Wilson
─See Page 23─

CRUNCHIE makes exciting biting! 4D

Above: The Daily Mirror front page on February 7, 1958

THE RACE FOR NO.19

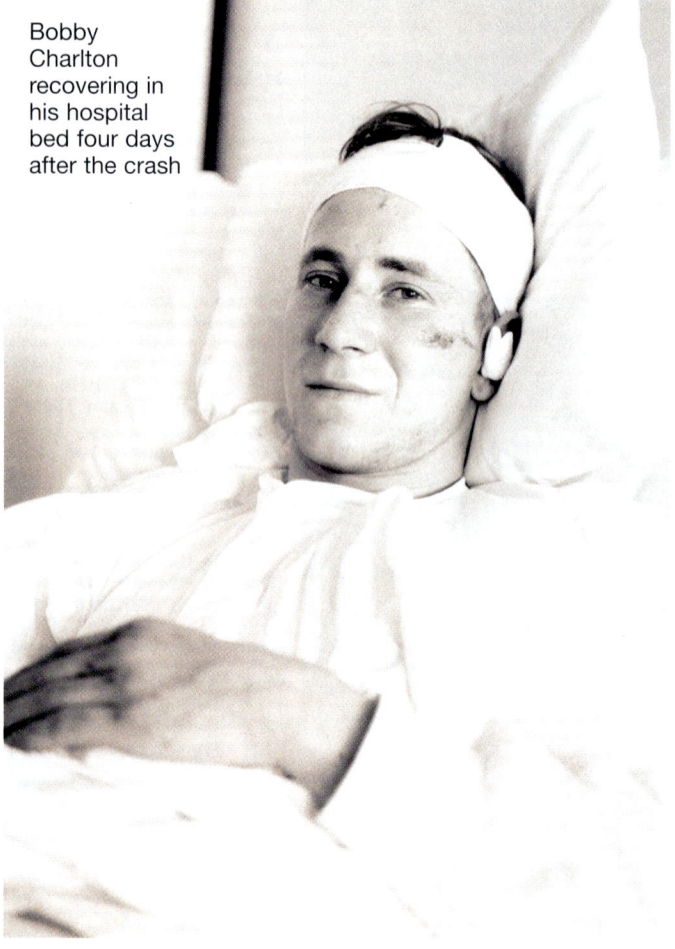

Jackie Blanchflower being treated in hospital. He never played again

Bobby Charlton recovering in his hospital bed four days after the crash

THE TEAM
IN THE PLANE CRASH
TRAGEDY

⬆ The last great match

THIS is a scene from Manchester United's last great match—just two days ago.

Bobby Charlton is seen scoring goal No. 2 in the 3—3 draw in Belgrade, Yugoslavia.

Last night Charlton was injured and in hospital after the tragic air crash at Munich, Germany, as the team flew home.

● Harry Gregg was United's dashing young goalkeeper when this picture was taken in Belgrade on Wednesday. Last night he lay injured in hospital. . . .

THE BUSBY BABES

DAILY MIRROR, Friday, February 7, 1958 . PAGE 13

EVERY one a star! These are the eleven players who have made Manchester United League Champions for two years.
DUNCAN EDWARDS. Left Half. Fate unknown.
BILL FOULKES. Right Back. Injured.
MARK JONES. Centre Half. Fate unknown.

RAY WOOD. Reserve goalkeeper. Seriously injured.
EDDIE COLMAN. Right Half. Fate unknown. Noted as a clever dribbler.
DAVID PEGG. Reserve Outside Left. Fate not known.
JOHN BERRY. Outside Right. Seriously injured. Bought from Birmingham

BILL WHELAN. Inside Forward. Fate unknown. An Eire international
ROGER BYRNE. England Left Back and Captain of United. Fate unknown.
TOMMY TAYLOR. England Centre Forward. Fate unknown.
DENIS VIOLLET. Inside Left. Seriously injured. United's top scorer

SWIFT	SCANLON	CHARLTON	GREGG	BENT	BLANCHFLOWER	MORGANS
killed	injured	injured	injured	injured	injured	injured
Frank Swift, the former England goalkeeper, had been reporting United's match for the News of World. He died in hospital last night.	Bert Scanlon is the local Manchester boy who made good. He recently established himself in the League side and was showing great promise.	Bobby Charlton, who is doing his Army call-up, is a nephew of famous former Newcastle forward Jackie Milburn. Bobby signed as a junior.	Harry Gregg, the world's most expensive goalkeeper, was recently bought from Doncaster Rovers for £23,000. The crowds thought him worth it.	Geoffrey Bent, reserve full back, who joined United as a junior. He was one of Busby's bright young men—all set to become a star of the future.	Jackie Blanchflower, Irish International centre half. He is a brother of Spurs' Danny Blanchflower, with whom he plays in Irish teams.	Ken Morgans, Welsh outside right from Swansea. He has only just established himself in the League side —another Busby new boy of promise.

The Mirror of February 7 provides the latest update on the condition of those involved in the crash. The final death toll was 23, eight of whom were Manchester United players. Those killed were: club captain Roger Byrne, Tommy Taylor, Duncan Edwards (15 days after the crash), David Pegg, Billy Whelan, Eddie Colman, Mark Jones and Geoff Bent

THE RACE FOR NO.19

Best, Law and Charlton

FORCED TO REBUILD AFTER THE SQUAD WAS SHORN OF SO MANY GREAT PLAYERS IN THE MUNICH AIR DISASTER, IT WASN'T LONG BEFORE MATT BUSBY LED MANCHESTER UNITED TO THE PINNACLE OF THE SPORT AGAIN, WITH SOME LEGENDARY NAMES BECOMING ICONS OF THE 1960S

Above: A new team emerges in March 1958. Back row: Bob Harrop, Ian Greaves, Freddie Goodwin, Harry Gregg, Stan Crowther, Ronnie Cope, Shay Brennan, Bill Inglis (reserve manager). Front row: Jack Compton (trainer), Alex Dawson, Mark Pearson, Bill Foulkes, Bobby Charlton, Ernie Taylor, Colin Webster

Left: Tired, muddy but elated at the end of the 1958 FA Cup semi-final replay at Highbury, a 5-3 win over Fulham which featured a hat-trick by Alex Dawson

BEST, LAW AND CHARLTON

Eyes on the action: Matt Busby watches his team closely during a game at Norwich in January 1959

Foot in the door: Denis Law is surrounded as he opens his shoe repair shop in Moston Lane, Blackley, Manchester, in March 1964

Derby joy: Bobby Charlton battles for the ball with Manchester City's Bill Leivers in February 1959, a year after Munich. United won the game 4-1

BEST, LAW AND CHARLTON

Left: The new cantilever stand at Old Trafford takes shape in March 1965

THE RACE FOR NO.19

"Pele wasn't as gifted as George Best and I would definitely put George above Johan Cruyff because he had more heart"

- Johnny Giles

Above: George Best is brought down by Liverpool goalkeeper Tommy Lawrence in April 1965. United won the game 3-0, a result that left them on the brink of becoming league champions

Right: Best, Nobby Stiles, Denis Law and David Herd are among United players celebrating in the bath after a 3-1 win over Arsenal sealed the league title

BEST, LAW AND CHARLTON

DAILY MIRROR, Tuesday, April 27, 1965

Manchester United champs..

'CRIPPLED' LAW THE HERO WITH TWO GOALS

Manchester United 3, Arsenal 1

MANCHESTER UNITED are champions again. That five-word sentence manager Matt Busby has waited seven years to read became a fact at 9.10 p.m. last night with the final whistle of Old Trafford's last home game.

But it was another minute of the tension that gripped the throat of everyone who watched or played before United and their fans could know it themselves—when the news came through that Leeds had only drawn at Birmingham.

It came over the same loudspeakers that throughout this match had acted as a lash, a spur and an inspiration to the Manchester United team on a night when both footballers and fans had to keep an anxious eye at the scoreboard of another game, ninety miles away.

Each time the score came over from Birmingham, the reaction from the eleven players that Busby has either bought for big money or has found and groomed with detailed care since the Munich crash was instant... violent... and dramatic.

Last night's triumph was shared equally between those very different men that Busby has welded into the best team in Britain.

It was Denis Law, the brightest of the big money men, who scored two United goals and created the other—even though his speed and mobility were both drastically reduced by the bandages protecting a cut under his knee still held together by stitches.

Yet, on this night Law, as an individual performer was matched and mastered by the home-grown talent around him.

By outstanding defenders like left back Tony Dunne and left half Nobby Stiles.

Icy Calm

And by that wispy waif on the left wing, little George Best, maintaining an incredible icy calm when more experienced men showed how the tension could cause talent to wither and wilt.

Here is the timetable of that tension:

7.37 p.m.—Seven minutes after the fierce start in which Arsenal had emphasised, by their determined attack, that the championship was too big a prize to be given away.

But United at last broke away and Law, twisting on that injured knee to avoid a tackle, slipped the ball to Best.

By FRANK McGHEE

The kid trapped it calmly, swivelled towards goal, paused almost cheekily to examine the situation, and then shot.

It looked near enough for goalkeeper Jim Furnell to dive at the ball.

But instead, Furnell made a feeble pass at it with his left foot, the ball struck his boot, bounced off and trickled over the line.

7.52 p.m.—The 22nd minute, and the news came through that Leeds were a goal down.

United immediately responded and Law shot inches high.

Yet, in fact, it was Arsenal who produced the more dangerous response with waves of attack that threatened to swamp United.

8.38—The 58th minute, and the news that Leeds were now three down produced instant success.

Hooked

Within 60 seconds, Furnell palmed David Herd's header on to the bar.

As the ball dropped Law was on it, bending his slim body backwards like a bow and hooking it in with his right foot.

8.47 p.m.—In the 67th minute. Arsenal pulled back to 2—1 with a penalty that provided its own small drama. Goalkeeper Pat Dunne parried George Eastham's first attempt with a brilliant dive, but was beaten when the England inside-left snapped up the rebound.

9.2 p.m.—In the 82nd minute, United, still being fiercely pressed back, heard that Leeds had pulled back to 3—2.

9.4 p.m.—In the 84th minute, United made certain of victory as Furnell, apparently unsighted, failed to gather the ball from a corner.

It dropped at Law's feet in front of an empty goal. He couldn't miss.

Yet it wasn't quite over... not until that 9.11 p.m. flash from Birmingham showed that United were champions again.

Denis Law, flanked by two Arsenal defenders, hooks in United's second goal after 59 minutes.

If only Villa could score nineteen..

MANCHESTER UNITED could still miss the First Division title... if Aston Villa beat them 19—0 in their last League game tomorrow! United and Leeds both have 61 points—and that's the fantastic score it would take now for Matt Busby's men to lose the title on goal average.

Chilly welcome as Hammers fly in

From KEN JONES Zaragoza, Monday.

WEST HAM arrived here tonight — to a chilly welcome. There was no welcoming committee and no battery of photographers, not one bouquet..

Hammers are here to meet Zaragoza in the second leg of their European Cup-Winners' Cup semi-final on Wednesday.

They hold a one-goal lead from the first leg at Upton Park three weeks ago... but they know they face what could be their toughest task yet.

THREE CRAVEN COTTAGE 'CHARACTERS' ARE AXED

By HARRY MILLER

FULHAM boss Vic Buckingham started a promised ten-player clear-out yesterday by giving free transfers to Maurice Cook, "Tosh" Chamberlain and Dave Underwood.

The trio of Craven Cottage "characters" were called into Buckingham's office and told they can go. The full list will be announced later this week.

Buckingham's decision to let centre forward Cook go without a fee is something of a shock.

He cost Fulham a £15,000 fee from Watford four years ago and has been a first team regular for much of this season. Reading are certain to show an interest.

Left winger Chamberlain, who has been out of action for the past ten weeks following a cartilage operation, will be ending a 15-year association with Fulham.

He told me last night: "I'm a bit choked. I understand the boss wants to cut the playing staff from 28 to 18. But because of my injury he hasn't seen me play since he took over."

Underwood, 36-year-old goalkeeper who has played for a string of clubs, joined Fulham two years ago. He said: "It seems the accent is going to be on youth at Fulham, so I'm out."

CLIFF MAY QUIT

Cliff Holton, 36-year-old Crystal Palace centre forward who was yesterday put on the transfer list, said yesterday that he may quit Soccer.

Above: The Daily Mirror hails the 1964/65 champions while, right, Denis Law is hoisted aloft by Herd and Bill Foulkes after the championship trophy was presented to the United squad

FINAL TABLE 1964/65

		Pld	W	D	L	F	A	GA	Pts
1	Manchester United	42	26	9	7	89	39	2.28	61
2	Leeds United	42	26	9	7	83	52	1.60	61
3	Chelsea	42	24	8	10	89	54	1.65	56
4	Everton	42	17	15	10	69	60	1.15	49
5	Nottingham Forest	42	17	13	12	71	67	1.06	47
6	Tottenham Hotspur	42	19	7	16	87	71	1.23	45
7	Liverpool	42	17	10	15	67	73	0.92	44
8	Sheffield Wednesday	42	16	11	15	57	55	1.04	43
9	West Ham United	42	19	4	19	82	71	1.16	42
10	Blackburn Rovers	42	16	10	16	83	79	1.05	42
11	Stoke City	42	16	10	16	67	66	1.01	42
12	Burnley	42	16	10	16	70	70	1.00	42
13	Arsenal	42	17	7	18	69	75	0.92	41
14	West Bromwich Albion	42	13	13	16	70	65	1.08	39
15	Sunderland	42	14	9	19	64	74	0.87	37
16	Aston Villa	42	16	5	21	57	82	0.69	37
17	Blackpool	42	12	11	19	67	78	0.86	35
18	Leicester City	42	11	13	18	69	85	0.81	35
19	Sheffield United	42	12	11	19	50	64	0.78	35
20	Fulham	42	11	12	19	60	78	0.77	34
21	Wolves	42	13	4	25	59	89	0.66	30
22	Birmingham City	42	8	11	23	64	96	0.67	27

THE RACE FOR NO.19

Above: Tempers are lost and Denis Law's shirt is ripped during the 1965 FA Cup semi-final against Leeds United. The Charlton brothers, on opposite sides, are in the thick of the flare-up

Below: Best, Law and Charlton, with the help of glamorous assistants, model coats at Old Trafford. Does it rain in Manchester?

Above: A Manchester United versus Manchester City Scalextric grand prix in November 1965

Opposite page: Bobby Charlton and Bobby Moore shake hands before a league match at Upton Park

"Charlton is a rarity, at one and the same time the architect who designs a game and the artist who adorns it"

– Michael Parkinson, 1968

THE RACE FOR NO.19

BEST, LAW AND CHARLTON

Champions salute: Matt Busby and his players applaud the Old Trafford crowd after receiving the league championship trophy in 1967. It would be another 26 years before the title was won again

THE RACE FOR NO.19

Above: A toast to the champions after a 6-1 win at West Ham confirmed United as the First Division league winners in 1967, while, left, the Mirror two days after the title was clinched. Jim McCalliog did sign for United but not until 1974

Below: Bobby Charlton receives his league championship winners' medal in 1967

FINAL TABLE 1966/67

		Pld	W	D	L	F	A	GA	Pts
1	Manchester United	42	24	12	6	84	45	1.87	60
2	Nottingham Forest	42	23	10	9	64	41	1.56	56
3	Tottenham Hotspur	42	24	8	10	71	48	1.48	56
4	Leeds United	42	22	11	9	62	42	1.48	55
5	Liverpool	42	19	13	10	64	47	1.36	51
6	Everton	42	19	10	13	65	46	1.41	48
7	Arsenal	42	16	14	12	58	47	1.23	46
8	Leicester City	42	18	8	16	78	71	1.10	44
9	Chelsea	42	15	14	13	67	62	1.08	44
10	Sheffield United	42	16	10	16	52	59	0.88	42
11	Sheffield Wednesday	42	14	13	15	56	47	1.19	41
12	Stoke City	42	17	7	18	63	58	1.09	41
13	West Bromwich Albion	42	16	7	19	77	73	1.05	39
14	Burnley	42	15	9	18	66	76	0.87	39
15	Manchester City	42	12	15	15	43	52	0.83	39
16	West Ham United	42	14	8	20	80	84	0.95	36
17	Sunderland	42	14	8	20	58	72	0.81	36
18	Fulham	42	11	12	19	71	83	0.86	34
19	Southampton	42	14	6	22	74	92	0.80	34
20	Newcastle United	42	12	9	21	39	81	0.48	33
21	Aston Villa	42	11	7	24	54	85	0.63	29
22	Blackpool	42	6	9	27	41	76	0.54	21

BEST, LAW AND CHARLTON

Head over heels: A spectacular volley from Denis Law against Tottenham in September 1967

Hunter and the hunted: George Best is chased by Norman Hunter in 1968

THE RACE FOR NO.19

DAILY MIRROR, Tuesday, May 14, 1968   PAGE 17

Profile

by
MICHAEL PARKINSON
OF THE SUNDAY TIMES

Once, in Lapland, I met a man wearing ear muffs and smelling strongly of reindeer. He knew only four words of English. They were: 'Bobby Charlton, number one'

AT THE age of thirty, Bobby Charlton would appear to have climbed every mountain.

He earns £10,000 a year, plays for Britain's most famous club, was in the team which won the World Cup at Wembley, and is without question the most respected footballer in the world.

People write to him and say: "Dear Bobby, I think you are great. I wish I was you...."

He has a lovely wife with a smile which stops you dead, a home in the Cheshire stockbroker belt, and a name which is known and admired in the farthest parts of this earth.

Once, in Lapland, I was approached by a man wearing ear muffs and smelling strongly of reindeer. He knew only four words of English. They were: "Bobby Charlton, number one," and he repeated them for hours with accompanying smiles of delight while we polished off a bottle of local firewater and watched the sun set over his reindeer.

But for all this fame and success, Bobby Charlton is still not completely fulfilled. He has one important ambition left—to be in the Manchester United team which wins the European Cup.

Tomorrow night in Madrid, in front of 130,000 noisy and exceedingly partisan Spaniards, he is hoping to play the sort of game which will win his team a place in the final and take him one step nearer the triumph which he and Matt Busby, the manager of Manchester United, want more than anything else in the world.

Charlton says: "We've got to win if only to see the look on the boss's face when we do it."

He is not being sloppy, simply underlining a deep relationship of respect and trust between himself and Busby. More than any other player in the team Charlton symbolises Busby's hopes and frustrations.

He was one of the famous Busby Babes, conceived and nursed by Busby and destroyed at Munich airport on their way home from a European Cup quarter-final—which they had won.

Charlton, like Busby, survived the crash, overcame the horror and became the foundation stone on which Busby built yet another great team.

Charlton thinks Busby is the greatest manager in the world. Busby thinks Charlton is the greatest player in the world. Few people would argue with either opinion.

When Bobby Charlton was born there was little doubt that he would be a

BOBBY CHARLTON by artist John Meyer

footballer. His mother, Cissie, is a member of Britain's most famous football family, the Milburns, of Ashington, Northumberland. He was a brilliant schoolboy footballer who turned down offers from a dozen top-class League clubs to join Manchester United on leaving school. He has been there ever since, learning his craft and learning it well enough to become what he is today, a master footballer.

Charlton is a rarity, at one and the same time the architect who designs a game and the artist who adorns it. He is one of that select band of footballers whose deeds are burned on the mind, one of the few who can bring a Press box full of journalists (who have seen most things) to their feet in unashamed admiration.

This season, against Southampton, he scored a goal of such speed and beauty that not one of the 50,000 crowd could possibly have seen the ball after it left his foot and before it magically appeared in the back of the net.

A journalist I knew shook his head in wonderment.

"By rights we can't report that goal," he said. I asked him what he meant. "Well, we're always told never to report what we don't see, and what proof have we that the ball now in the net is the same one which left Charlton's foot."

He doesn't look a thoroughbred when he steps on to a field. At first glance you'd imagine him suited more to donkey work than artistic endeavour.

The trunk is sturdy and made for stamina, the legs are fearsome, resembling those which are normally employed holding up billiards tables. But in action he is beautiful. There is no other word. On the ball and in full flight he is the most noble sight in football, a superb blend of grace and athleticism, delicacy and power.

FOR a man who can make people's spines tingle, he is remarkably undemonstrative. He gets very pink-faced and Anglo-Saxon during the ritual cuddling which follows one of his goals.

His modesty is alarming and the despair of sports journalists eager for the revealing quote.

Some time ago, after two wonderful displays against Benfica in the European Cup, Charlton received rave write-ups. Bela Guttman, one of the most knowledgeable men in football, said that if Benfica had Charlton they would win the World Cup, never mind the European competition.

Charlton was pressed for his reaction to this mountain of praise. Wasn't he thrilled, elated by what people said? He thought for a moment and replied: "They are entitled to their opinions."

This reluctance to believe what people said about him gained Charlton the false reputation of being dour and moody. That was some time ago, before people realised that he was simply an exceedingly modest young man.

But for all his skill as a player and all his modesty as a man, Charlton has won his biggest following for his exemplary behaviour on the field. In an age when many footballers mix the petulance of spoiled brats with the physical approach of night club bouncers, Bobby Charlton is a shining example of controlled professionalism.

If he is as much as talked to by a referee, it is an event rare enough to make the headlines. When he is felled by an opponent, as he often is, he allows himself a pitying glance at the offender. Nothing more.

When others jostle the referee, questioning his authority, Charlton walks away, accepting the decision quietly no matter how ludicrous it might have been. He has the priceless quality of self-control which in the final analysis is that which separates the great sportsmen from those who are simply very good.

In an age of whizz-kids and swingers and Flash Harrys, there is something reassuring about Bobby Charlton. He stands for those old-fashioned virtues of good manners and unassuming charm which the post-war generations have supposedly scrapped.

DURING the World Cup, when because of television, footballers reached a totally new audience, it was Bobby Charlton the mums adored.

They would write to him and say: "Dear Bobby, I think you are very nice and I wish I had a son like you."

Today Bobby Charlton is a very solid citizen, calmly scanning the horizon, thinking only about playing football.

He reckons he has a good few years left in him yet, and won't even contemplate what he might do when he eventually retires.

"I refuse to think about retiring. When you start thinking along those lines then you're on your way out," he says.

In the frenetic world of football Bobby Charlton is a serene figure unaffected by the adoration of his fans, content just to be very good at his job.

Those who admire him can also look forward without concern to the future years, because they know that although their idol might lose his form, he will never fall from grace.

Opposite, top: Bobby Charlton and Matt Busby face some young competition during a game of street football. Below them, George Best fires in a shot against Ipswich in November 1968

Above: Three years before his television chatshow began, and ahead of the 1968 European Cup final, this Michael Parkinson profile of Bobby Charlton was reproduced in the Daily Mirror

THE RACE FOR NO.19

Above: Best, Pat Crerand, Frank McLintock and John Radford are all airborne during a United-Arsenal clash from October 1967

Right: George inspects his European Footballer of the Year award in 1969, watched by Bobby Charlton, Matt Busby and Denis Law

Above: John Aston senior demands a series of sit-ups at United's old training ground, The Cliff, in 1969. His son, John junior, Best and Law are among the players crunching their stomachs

Left: Matt Busby at his desk in May 1968, the month his team won the European Cup, 10 years after Munich

"Perhaps Sir Matt's greatest achievement was that he made Manchester United a way of life for people"

- Sir Bobby Charlton

THE RACE FOR NO.19

The Barren Years

AFTER THE HIGHS OF THE '50S AND '60S, THE QUEST FOR FURTHER TITLES IN THE '70S AND '80S FELL FLAT WITH UNITED SUFFERING THE IGNOMINY OF RELEGATION TO THE SECOND DIVISION. A SILVER LINING WAS PROVIDED WITH CUP SUCCESSES ALONG THE WAY

Curtain call: Camera crews capture Bobby Charlton as he walks onto the pitch for his final Manchester United game at Chelsea in April 1973

On a different plane: George Best left United in January 1974. By the end of that season, they were a Second Division club

THE BARREN YEARS

The mighty have fallen: February 1975 and United are at the Manor Ground, Oxford, for a Second Division fixture. Lou Macari is pictured attempting an overhead kick

Cup that cheers: The United bench rise to celebrate Norman Whiteside's winning goal in the 1985 FA Cup final. Although manager Ron Atkinson, **below**, couldn't lead United to a league title, he did preside over FA Cup wins in 1983 and 1985

"Bryan Robson has all the qualities you expect of a captain. He is our most complete player. Bryan can win the ball and score. What more can you ask for?"

– England manager Bobby Robson after handing his namesake the captaincy in September 1982

THE BARREN YEARS

Party trick: Bryan Robson celebrates his goal in the victory over Arsenal in March 1984 by kicking his boot in the air

THE RACE FOR NO.19

The Premier Team

SINCE THE PREMIER LEAGUE WAS CREATED IN 1992/93, MANCHESTER UNITED HAVE DOMINATED DOMESTIC FOOTBALL IN ENGLAND. UNDER THE MANAGEMENT OF SIR ALEX FERGUSON, THEY HAVE CLAIMED AN INCREDIBLE 11 OF THE 17 TITLES AVAILABLE

Opposite: Daily Mirror back pages marking United's first four Premier League triumphs

Left: Steve Bruce and Bryan Robson celebrate with the trophy after United claimed the first Premier League trophy - ending a wait of 26 years for a top-flight title

THE RACE FOR NO.19

PAGE 30 DAILY MIRROR, Tuesday, May 4, 1993

IT'S GOLD TRAFFORD AS TH

GLORY

Reds' party night

➡ **From Back Page**

who started the Old Trafford party night when he was presented with the Barclays Manager of the Month award, was clearly overcome by the incredible show of emotion and relief from over 40,000 fans packed into the ground.

● He declared: "This is a wonderful night. You strive all through your life to get the kind of feeling we have now."

● Ferguson proclaimed his £1million buy Eric Cantona as the player who had provided the missing link to the title.

● Fergie stressed: "Eric illuminated the stadium. The players all responded to his imagination and flair."

● George Best, one of Old Trafford's living legends, singled out Ryan Giggs as the man who can spark an Anfield-style domination of the game in the decade to come.

● Best insisted: "Ryan has got everything. He could turn into one of the greatest ever."

● Giggs, who found the equaliser last

FINAL TABLE 1992/93

		Pld	W	D	L	F	A	GD	Pts
1	Manchester United	42	24	12	6	67	31	36	84
2	Aston Villa	42	21	11	10	57	40	17	74
3	Norwich City	42	21	9	12	61	65	-4	72
4	Blackburn Rovers	42	20	11	11	68	46	22	71
5	Queens Park Rangers	42	17	12	13	63	55	8	63
6	Liverpool	42	16	11	15	62	55	7	59
7	Sheffield Wednesday	42	15	14	13	55	51	4	59
8	Tottenham Hotspur	42	16	11	15	60	66	-6	59
9	Manchester City	42	15	12	15	56	51	5	57
10	Arsenal	42	15	11	16	40	38	2	56
11	Chelsea	42	14	14	14	51	54	-3	56
12	Wimbledon	42	14	12	16	56	55	1	54
13	Everton	42	15	8	19	53	55	-2	53
14	Sheffield United	42	14	10	18	54	53	1	52
15	Coventry City	42	13	13	16	52	57	-5	52
16	Ipswich Town	42	12	16	14	50	55	-5	52
17	Leeds United	42	12	15	15	57	62	-5	51
18	Southampton	42	13	11	18	54	61	-7	50
19	Oldham Athletic	42	13	10	19	63	74	-11	49
20	Crystal Palace	42	11	16	15	48	61	-13	49
21	Middlesbrough	42	11	11	20	54	75	-21	44
22	Nottingham Forest	42	10	10	22	41	62	-21	40

SILVER LINING

BOY wonder Ryan Giggs holds the Premier League trophy aloft on another night of personal glory – while boss Alex Ferguson is keen to get his hands on the Cup.

MAN

DAILY MIRROR, Tuesday, May 4, 1993 PAGE 31

CHAMPS CELEBRATE IN STYLE

GLORY

1ST CHAMPION: The United first team squad stage their own knees-up after a scintillating display victory over Blackburn

Pictures: ALBERT COOPER

OLD TRAFFORD rocked in a frenzy of colourful celebration last night – and centre stage it was simply red.

The party began with the sound of "Glory, Glory Man United," ripping through the stadium. And a full house turned up the volume as their heroes paraded with the style that had ended a quarter of a century's agonising wait for the League title.

It was like a Beatles concert and The Last Night of the Proms rolled into one. "Absolutely fantastic," said Bobby Charlton, a reminder of United's great days of the '60s. "I can't remember a night as noisy, as colourful. It was just too memorable for words."

His ears were still ringing long after the time when the champagne began to flow And with the sort of fanatical following that turned the ground into an echo chamber last night, they'll be spurred on to even greater glories than 1968 when they won the European Cup.

Anyone who doubts what this eighth title means to United should have spent the day around Old Trafford.

The fans had massed since mid-morning; whole families strolled round the stadium with babes in arms, toddlers in push chairs, aunts and grannies dressed in replica kit, everyone wanting to share the moment.

It was a magical, unforgettable day and the crowds were so massive outside they had to open the gates two hours before the kick-off to let the fans in.

Thousands without tickets had to be content to taste second-hand the festivities winding to a crescendo as the kick-off approached.

Inside the ground the first giant roar greeted George Best and Denis Law — reminders of that last golden era.

But the party began in earnest with the announcement of the team, followed by their emergence for the warm-up wearing an assortment of championship tee-shirts, hastily collected from the hawkers outside.

There was no holding back now as 40,000 burst into song and on the celebrations went with Charlton, another of the last championship-winning team, presenting the reserve and young players of the year with their awards.

Then the man of the moment appeared. Boss Alex Ferguson collected his Barclays "Manager of the Month" award and the roof on England's most spectacular stadium bowed towards the sky.

But Blackburn were in no mood to celebrate United's success — and they hit Old Trafford with a gate crasher of a goal from Kevin Gallacher after only 10 minutes.

Shining

It only served to fire the United fans into a frenzy of sound that lifted Fergie's lads.

And wonder-boy Ryan Giggs started the celebrations all over again with a memorable free-kick.

Paul Ince made it 2-1 and, with the last kick of the game, Gary Pallister, United's most expensive player, did his party piece from a free-kick and made it 3-1.

Twenty United players had been used to recapture the long-lost top division title — and the 16 who qualified for their shining bit of history at the end of the game.

Ferguson sent skipper Steve Bruce and United's favourite hero Bryan Robson up the rostrum together to collect the inaugural Premier League Trophy.

They stood side-by-side triumphantly holding aloft the £20,000, 30-inch high Cup that had cost £22million for Manchester United to win.

There were no medals — instead the Premier League awarded miniature replicas of the magnificent trophy to each of the players.

The club banked £815,000 for clinching the title — and now United face the greatest bonanza in their history.

There's more — much more — to come with a guaranteed £3million if they make it to the European semi-finals.

Tickets will become like gold dust. Last night they changed hands, if you could persuade a fan to part, for as much as £250.

But there was nobody who would have felt cheated if they had paid that much to be present on such a memorable occasion.

Fergie said later: "I know Bobby Charlton has called Old Trafford the Dream Theatre — and nothing could beat that description tonight."

He wrote his own history-making chapter in the football record books.

He's the only manager to take a treble in both the English the Scottish leagues with Cup, European Cup and League titles.

Since he was appointed in November 1986, he had his steely eyes set on taking United into Europe as English champions.

And the crowd last night never let him forget their gratitude.

They all went home hoarse — and if the Manchester Ship Canal had been best bitter, they'd have drunk it dry in celebration.

Fans pump up the volume for heroes

By TED MACAULEY: Man Utd 3, Blackburn 1

UTD

CHARLTON: FANTAS

MAN of the CENTU

'Alex can keep u top u the yea

By KEN LAWRENCE

BOBBY CHARLTON finds it hard to keep himself from smirking these days. Tougher still to resist the temptation to say: "I told you so!"

For it was the World Cup legend who persuaded the Manchester United board to hire Alex Ferguson.

Now, seven-and-a-half years on from the grey day that Fergie arrived at Old Trafford, United have not only exorcised the championship curse but have won the title for a second successive time.

Trophies

Indeed, if United can beat Chelsea in the FA Cup final on Saturday, they will have amassed seven trophies in four years and Ferguson will have achieved something even Sir Matt Busby could not do — complete the double.

Charlton last night paid tribute to the manager who simply refused to let the enormity of the job at Manchester United ruin his vision of a brave new world.

Charlton insisted: "I believe we are now on course to stay as England's dominant force way past the Year 2000 — and that is down to Alex.

"He has shown incredible self-belief, great personal resilience, tactical awareness — and just would not allow himself to be deflected. Now we are reaping the rewards of Alex's master plan. Something that took quite some time to come together. Now everything's in place for us to go on winning trophies year after year after year."

Following the retirement of Busby in 1969, five managers had stumbled in their quest for the title.

Until he won the FA Cup in 1990, Fergie looked like following Wilf McGuinness, Frank O'Farrell, Tommy Docherty, Dave Sexton and Ron Atkinson down the same road to nowhere.

Course

Yet Charlton insists: "Personally I never had any doubts about what Alex could achieve with us — and by the time we won at Wembley in 1990 I reckon he was bang on course.

"I know people had been calling for his head, but as a board of directors we decided that when we appointed Alex we were going to give him the time he needed — no matter what.

"Yes, it was me who persuaded Martin Edwards and the rest to talk to Alex. And I'm proud of that — espepcialy with the way things have gone.

"I've always believed he would crack it here. But the credit goes to only one person — Alex Ferguson, because he is the man who has made it all work."

Charlton became convinced that Ferguson was the only man to lift United out of their latest crisis the moment he met him for the first time.

"He was desperate for the job. He couldn't wait," said Charlton. "Because for him managing Manchester United was the ultimate challenge.

"There was no fear in him, no worry that having become such a big name in Scotland with Aberdeen it would all go wrong down here. I don't think Alex

THE PREMIER TEAM

...TIC FERGIE...

...s at the ...til past ...r 2000!'

...ctually realised just how big the challenge was, however, nor how big the club actually is.

"But he wasn't afraid of it. He got down to business, put together his long-term plan and got on with it, sometimes working 20 hours a day, day after day.

"One of the problems, in fact, is calming Alex down, making him take a break. It's just about impossible!

Dinner

"Sometimes you can drag him out for dinner, or maybe on to the golf course.

"But it doesn't make much difference — all he wants to do is talk about United, anyway. His mind is never off it.

"Yet these demands are not from the club. Alex puts those demands on himself.

"I see him just keeping on going. Well past the turn of the century, because I believe the team he has put together now is as good as the one we had back in the Sixties."

JUST CHAMPION: Alex Ferguson gets his hands on the Premiership trophy for the second season running.

Left: Sir Bobby Charlton's comments after the May 1994 title win proved prophetic!

FINAL TABLE 1993/94

		Pld	W	D	L	F	A	GD	Pts
1	Manchester United	42	27	11	4	80	38	42	92
2	Blackburn Rovers	42	25	9	8	63	36	27	84
3	Newcastle United	42	23	8	11	82	41	41	77
4	Arsenal	42	18	17	7	53	28	25	71
5	Leeds United	42	18	16	8	65	39	26	70
6	Wimbledon	42	18	11	13	56	53	3	65
7	Sheffield Wednesday	42	16	16	10	76	54	22	64
8	Liverpool	42	17	9	16	59	55	4	60
9	Queens Park Rangers	42	16	12	14	62	61	1	60
10	Aston Villa	42	15	12	15	46	50	-4	57
11	Coventry City	42	14	14	14	43	45	-2	56
12	Norwich City	42	12	17	13	65	61	4	53
13	West Ham United	42	13	13	16	47	58	-11	52
14	Chelsea	42	13	12	17	49	53	-4	51
15	Tottenham Hotspur	42	11	12	19	54	59	-5	45
16	Manchester City	42	9	18	15	38	49	-11	45
17	Everton	42	12	8	22	42	63	-21	44
18	Southampton	42	12	7	23	49	66	-17	43
19	Ipswich Town	42	9	16	17	35	58	-23	43
20	Sheffield United	42	8	18	16	42	60	-18	42
21	Oldham Athletic	42	9	13	20	42	68	-26	40
22	Swindon Town	42	5	15	22	47	100	-53	30

FINAL TABLE 1995/96

		Pld	W	D	L	F	A	GD	Pts
1	Manchester United	38	25	7	6	73	35	38	82
2	Newcastle United	38	24	6	8	66	37	29	78
3	Liverpool	38	20	11	7	70	34	36	71
4	Aston Villa	38	18	9	11	52	35	17	63
5	Arsenal	38	17	12	9	49	32	17	63
6	Everton	38	17	10	11	64	44	20	61
7	Blackburn Rovers	38	18	7	13	61	47	14	61
8	Tottenham Hotspur	38	16	13	9	50	38	12	61
9	Nottingham Forest	38	15	13	10	50	54	-4	58
10	West Ham United	38	14	9	15	43	52	-9	51
11	Chelsea	38	12	14	12	46	44	2	50
12	Middlesbrough	38	11	10	17	35	50	-15	43
13	Leeds United	38	12	7	19	40	57	-17	43
14	Wimbledon	38	10	11	17	55	70	-15	41
15	Sheffield Wednesday	38	10	10	18	48	61	-13	40
16	Coventry City	38	8	14	16	42	60	-18	38
17	Southampton	38	9	11	18	34	52	-18	38
18	Manchester City	38	9	11	18	33	58	-25	38
19	Queens Park Rangers	38	9	6	23	38	57	-19	33
20	Bolton Wanderers	38	8	5	25	39	71	-32	29

59

THE RACE FOR NO.19

Peter Schmeichel

"I know I am part of the great United side of all time. If we played the '68 team now we would beat them 10-0. Since the '60s everything has changed in football. The pace of the game is so much faster.

Just look at the old videos and see the space they had and the time they had on the ball. That doesn't happen any more. We probably play at twice the speed they did in '68.

That's why I'm saying we would beat them. I am not saying that they were not a great team in their own time. They were a fantastic side. But times have changed. In 1968 it was a different world. Probably a better one. Things have moved on, though."

George Best

"I don't think there will ever be a better side than United back in 1968 and nothing will ever make me change my mind.

I'm totally biased but we are the better side. There'd be a few goals in it because we used to play five up front. There'd be myself, Charlton, Kidd, Aston and Crerand running at them.

Even with modern tactics we'd still beat them and I think we'd do it comfortably too.

You have to remember that we had three European Player of the Years in our team. Denis won it in 1964. Bobby in '66 and I won it in 1968 and I don't think that will ever happen again.

I've never seen anyone from the 1968 team saying that this current team is better and that doesn't surprise me. Every time we went out on the pitch, I thought we were unbeatable."

FINAL TABLE 1996/97

		Pld	W	D	L	F	A	GD	Pts
1	Manchester United	38	21	12	5	76	44	32	75
2	Newcastle United	38	19	11	8	73	40	33	68
3	Arsenal	38	19	11	8	62	32	30	68
4	Liverpool	38	19	11	8	62	37	25	68
5	Aston Villa	38	17	10	11	47	34	13	61
6	Chelsea	38	16	11	11	58	55	3	59
7	Sheffield Wednesday	38	14	15	9	50	51	-1	57
8	Wimbledon	38	15	11	12	49	46	3	56
9	Leicester City	38	12	11	15	46	54	-8	47
10	Tottenham Hotspur	38	13	7	18	44	51	-7	46
11	Leeds United	38	11	13	14	28	38	-10	46
12	Derby County	38	11	13	14	45	58	13	46
13	Blackburn Rovers	38	9	15	14	42	43	-1	42
14	West Ham United	38	10	12	16	39	48	-9	42
15	Everton	38	10	12	16	44	57	-13	42
16	Southampton	38	10	11	17	50	56	-6	41
17	Coventry City	38	9	14	15	38	54	-16	41
18	Sunderland	38	10	10	18	35	53	-18	40
19	Middlesbrough	38	10	12	16	51	60	-9	39
20	Nottingham Forest	38	6	16	16	31	59	-28	34

"He is the player we all looked up to and the player the other teams feared - and they did fear him"

— Gary Neville on Eric Cantona

"The years of Eric Cantona have been great. He has been a model professional and a joy to manage. He's certainly one of the most gifted and dedicated players that I've ever had the pleasure of working with. Whenever fans discuss United's greatest-ever side, you can be sure that for many, Eric's name will be very high on the list"

– Sir Alex Ferguson

MirrorSport

MANCHESTER UNITED TAKE FIRST STEP TO TREBLE

CHAMPIONS

By STEVE MILLAR

OLD TRAFFORD messiah Alex Ferguson last night praised his young "gods" for putting him on the brink of treble immortality.

Manchester United's triumph over Tottenham at Old Trafford meant Ferguson collected his fifth title in seven spectacular years.

But he was the first to thank his players for earning him his 11th major honour in English football and Ferguson talked, too, of the great man who made it all possible – Sir Matt Busby.

Ferguson, whose success equalled Sir Matt's own championship record, could not hide his delight. He danced on the pitch with his celebrating players and said: "I know I am starting to print my players as gods, but it is

TURN TO PAGE 39

HOW THEY FINISHED

	P	W	D	L	F	A	Pts
Man Utd	38	22	13	3	80	37	79
Arsenal	38	22	12	4	59	17	78
Chelsea	38	20	15	3	57	30	75
Leeds	38	18	13	7	62	34	67

THE AGONY AND THE ECSTASY: Arsene Wenger is mortified while Manchester United players celebrate (main picture)

PETER THE GREATEST SEE PAGES 36 & 37

COLE HITS THE GOLDEN GOAL SEE PAGES 38 & 39

ARSENAL IN AGONY MANIA PAGES 2 & 3

INSIDE: ALL THE DRAMA IN YOUR Mania PULL-OUT *Plus Man Utd poster*

Left: Beckham, Keane, Solskjaer, Cole and Giggs celebrate a dramatic late FA Cup win over Liverpool in 1999

Opposite: Taking the first step to a historic treble in 1999

Below: Dwight Yorke salutes the crowds during the open top bus parade to celebrate United's 1999 treble of Premier League, FA Cup and Champions League

FINAL TABLE 1998/99

		Pld	W	D	L	F	A	GD	Pts
1	Manchester United	38	22	13	3	80	37	43	79
2	Arsenal	38	22	12	4	59	17	42	78
3	Chelsea	38	20	15	3	57	30	27	75
4	Leeds United	38	18	13	7	62	34	28	67
5	West Ham United	38	16	9	13	46	53	-7	57
6	Aston Villa	38	15	10	13	51	46	5	55
7	Liverpool	38	15	9	14	68	49	19	54
8	Derby County	38	13	13	12	40	45	-5	52
9	Middlesbrough	38	12	15	11	48	54	-6	51
10	Leicester City	38	12	13	13	40	46	-6	49
11	Tottenham Hotspur	38	11	14	13	47	50	-3	47
12	Sheffield Wednesday	38	13	7	18	41	42	-1	46
13	Newcastle United	38	11	13	14	48	54	-6	46
14	Everton	38	11	10	17	42	47	-5	43
15	Coventry City	38	11	9	18	39	51	-12	42
16	Wimbledon	38	10	12	16	40	63	-23	42
17	Southampton	38	11	8	19	37	64	-27	41
18	Charlton Athletic	38	8	12	18	41	56	-15	36
19	Blackburn Rovers	38	7	14	17	38	52	-14	35
20	Nottingham Forest	38	7	9	22	35	69	-34	30

THE RACE FOR NO.19

PAGE 78 SUNDAY MIRROR, April 23, 2000 LOLA

MILLENNIUM CHAMPIONS – IT'S

KING FERGIE

DELL JOY: David Beckham

Ferguson salutes his 'best ever'

From Back Page

occasions and great success, too. We played 14 matches in Europe this season – more than we played last season when we won the trophy.

"We had to get over the disappointment of losing to Madrid, but at this club, there is always another big match coming up to focus on – and that was the case at Southampton.

"I think this is a maturing team – they are just getting better all the time. The great thing is that the longer teams stay together and grow together, the better they become."

Ferguson also paid tribute to Liverpool manager Gerard Houllier for creating a team which clearly is going to be a threat next season.

Fergie said of United's challengers: "I'm surprised Chelsea, who we play on Monday, haven't been closer to us. At the start of the season I thought Arsenal, Chelsea and Leeds would be our main challengers.

"I thought it would take Liverpool time with all the changes there, but Gerard has done a fantastic job. They are the form team.

"Mind you, we were cheering for Everton on Friday night – and they did the business for us!

"Then we got the start we wanted against Southampton, and to go three up gave us a nice cushion.

"Now we have set a target to win all of the last four

MANCHESTER DELL-IGHTED: Ole Gunnar Solskjaer shows champion form as he gets the better of Dean Richards to fire number three for United at Southampton — and (left) Phil Neville is well pleased with his contribution to Francis Benali's own goal which had made it two

SOUTHAMPTON 1 MAN UTD 3

11	Fouls committed	8
2	Yellow cards	1
0	Red cards	0
1	Offside	3
2	Corners	7
8	Shots on target	9
4	Shots off target	5

By PAUL SMITH

MANCHESTER United took just 29 minutes to wrap up their sixth Premiership title in eight seasons.

A devastating first half display on the south coast ensured United retained their crown as goals from David Beckham and Ole Gunnar Solskjaer sandwiching a Francis Benali own-goal, blew poor Southampton away at The Dell.

Any fears that United would suffer from nerves in a week when they were dumped out of the European Cup were dispelled inside seven minutes by a trademark Beckham free-kick.

Then Benali put through his own net after Phil Neville's low, driven cross in the 15th minute, and 14 minutes later the title was on its way back to Old Trafford as Solskjaer added a third.

United boss Sir Alex Ferguson had watched in despair as his side were torn apart by Real Madrid at Old Trafford on Wednesday, and stated his intent by immediately splashing out £19million on Dutch striker Ruud van Nistelrooy.

United could have bought four Southampton teams for the price of van Nistelrooy, bearing in mind Saints were assembled for a mere £4.5m.

But while the gulf in class appeared immeasurable, it didn't give United any divine right to victory.

United made four sweeping changes from the team that crashed out of Europe in midweek. In came Phil Neville, Mikael Silvestre, Solskjaer and Nicky Butt.

United had made it clear that, whatever the result at The Dell, they would not pick up the Premiership trophy until their last home game of the season against Spurs on May 6.

But one wag wondered whether it would save time if they were presented with it on the day of their FIRST home game instead.

United clearly meant business and were in no mood to put their celebrations on hold until tomorrow's televised clash with Chelsea at Old Trafford.

Seven minutes in, Andy Cole was brought down on the edge of the area by Benali's poorly timed tackle.

Cue Beckham from 25 yards. Saints reserve

FINAL TABLE 1999/00

		Pld	W	D	L	F	A	GD	Pts
1	Manchester United	38	28	7	3	97	45	52	91
2	Arsenal	38	22	7	9	73	43	30	73
3	Leeds United	38	21	6	11	58	43	15	69
4	Liverpool	38	19	10	9	51	30	21	67
5	Chelsea	38	18	11	9	53	34	19	65
6	Aston Villa	38	15	13	10	46	35	11	58
7	Sunderland	38	16	10	12	57	56	1	58
8	Leicester City	38	16	7	15	55	55	0	55
9	West Ham United	38	15	10	13	52	53	-1	55
10	Tottenham Hotspur	38	15	8	15	57	49	8	53
11	Newcastle United	38	14	10	14	63	54	9	52
12	Middlesbrough	38	14	10	14	46	52	-6	52
13	Everton	38	12	14	12	59	49	10	50
14	Coventry City	38	12	8	18	47	54	-7	44
15	Southampton	38	12	8	18	45	62	-17	44
16	Derby County	38	9	11	18	44	57	-13	38
17	Bradford City	38	9	9	20	38	68	-30	36
18	Wimbledon	38	7	12	19	46	74	-28	33
19	Sheffield Wednesday	38	8	7	23	38	70	-32	31
20	Watford	38	6	6	26	35	77	-42	24

SUNDAY MIRROR, April 23, 2000 PAGE 79

UNITED'S SIXTH PREMIER LEAGUE TITLE

THE SIXTH

Brilliant Beckham starts the party as mighty United enjoy a glorious day at the seaside

eeper Neil Moss had no ance as the ball bent und the wall to spark early United celebrations.
Eight minutes later Phil eville galloped down the t and as the Southampton fence backed off, his low oss was turned into his wn goal by Benali.
The recalled Saints defender was having a nightmare. But his blushes were ared in the 20th minute by oss. Solskjaer closed Benali down, won possession d let fly in an instant. ly to see Moss tip the ball way.
But in the 29th minute nited added a clinching ird. Roy Keane laid the ll off to Beckham, and his -yard sweeping pass found olskjaer, whose cross-shot ve Moss no chance.
Beckham, given free-kick actice by Southampton, uld have grabbed his second, but for once his trusty ght foot let him down and e Saints wall took the full rce of his shot.
The game threatened to ow up after the break. eane was booked after ying into Chris Marsden r a late challenge on eckham and a minute later evin Davies received a ellow card for another asty tackle on the England idfielder.
The threat of a Southampton revival was unlikely nd Ferguson replaced iggs, bringing on Ronny ohnsen for his first game of e season following surgery n both his knees last year. Matthew Le Tissier was rought on in the 71st inute to inject some rgency into the Southamp-

ton side, while at the same time Dwight Yorke and Teddy Sheringham replaced Solskjaer and Cole.
Even so, United were simply going through the motions. There were times when they looked capable of snatching another goal, but little to suggest they were too concerned.
Six minutes from time Marian Pahars pulled a goal back for the home side. But by the time it found the back of the net, United had already started celebrating.

STAR MAN: David Beckham. Scored one, created another as United partied on the South Coast.
SOUTHAMPTON: Moss 8, Dodd 7, Benali 5 (Kachloul 6), El Khalej 6, Richards 6, Lundekvam 6, Marsden 6, Pahars 6, Davies 5, Tessem 6, Bridge 6.
MAN UTD: Van der Gouw 7, G Neville 7, P Neville 7, Stam 7, Silvestre 7, BECKHAM 9, Keane 8, Solskjaer 8 (Yorke 6), Cole 7 (Sheringham 6), Butt 7, Giggs 7 (Johnsen 7).
MANAGERS: Hoddle 5; Ferguson 8.
REFEREE: N Barry 8.

TOP OF THE PREMIERSHIP

	P	W	D	L	F	A	Pt
Man Utd	34	24	7	3	87	40	79
Liverpool	34	19	9	6	51	25	66
Arsenal	32	18	6	8	60	32	60
Leeds	33	19	3	11	49	39	60
Chelsea	34	16	11	7	44	29	59

GAMES TO PLAY
MAN UTD
Apr 24 Chelsea (h); Apr 29 Watford (a); May 6 Tottenham (h); May 14 Aston Villa(a)
SOUTHAMPTON
Apr 24 Derby (a); Apr 29 Leicester (h); May 7 Liverpool (a); May 14 Wimbledon (h)

BECK AND HAUL: Beckham fires the first and Yorke hails victory

Vialli: Reds are out of this world

GIANLUCA VIALLI last night admitted that Manchester United are in a league of their own.
The Chelsea manager said: "United deserve credit and it's fair that they have won the title because they are the best team and have been so consistent this season.
"They are out of everybody's league and we have to improve to bridge the gap."
At Tottenham STEWART HOUSTON said: "I would like to wish Alex well. He telephoned in the week to see how George Graham was, so I am pleased for him. It is a wonderful achievement."
West Ham boss HARRY REDKNAPP was also full of praise, saying: "This has been another magnificent season for Manchester United. I take my hat off to Alex Ferguson and his squad – again.
"They have been favourites to win the title from day one and it is no surprise to me that they have clinched it with room to spare.
"I think Arsenal and possibly Liverpool will be strong next season, but it's hard to see anyone ending United's dominance just yet."
Coventry skipper GARY McALLISTER said: "I'm not surprised that they have clinched the title so soon because, quite simply, they are the best team by a long way.
"The thing about them is that they rarely, if ever, have any freak results go against them – and they always win the games you expect them to win."
Aston Villa boss JOHN GREGORY insisted: "If we are all not careful United will keep winning the title by Easter!"

How the top five's fortunes fluctuated

HOW UNITED WON THE TITLE

Date	Opponents	Score	Scorers	Crowd	Date	Opponents	Score	Scorers	Crowd
Aug 8	A Everton	1-1	Yorke 7	39,141	Dec 26	H Bradford	4-0	Fortune 75, Yorke 79, Cole 87, Keane 88	55,188
Aug 11	H Sheff Wed	4-0	Scholes 9, Yorke 35, Cole 54, Solskjaer 84	54,941	Dec 28	A Sunderland	2-2	Keane 27, Butt 86	42,026
Aug 14	H Leeds Utd	2-0	Yorke 76 80	55,187	Jan 24	H Arsenal	1-1	Sheringham 73	58,293
Aug 22	A Arsenal	2-1	Keane 58 88	38,147	Jan 29	A Boro	1-0	Beckham 87	61,267
Aug 25	A Coventry	2-1	Scholes 62 Yorke 75	22,024	Feb 2	H Sheff Wed	1-0	Sheringham 73	39,640
Aug 30	H Newcastle	5-1	Cole 14 46 65 71, Giggs 80	55,190	Feb 5	H Coventry	3-2	Cole 39, 54 Scholes 77	61,380
Sep 11	A Liverpool	3-2	Carragher (og) 3, (og) 44, Cole 18	44,929	Feb 12	A Newcastle	0-3		36,476
Sep 18	H Wimbledon	1-1	Cruyff 73	55,789	Feb 20	A Leeds Utd	1-0	Cole 51	40,160
Sep 25	H Southampton	3-3	Sheringham 34, Yorke 37 64	55,249	Feb 26	A Wimbledon	2-2	Cruyff 30, Cole 90	26,129
Oct 3	A Chelsea	0-5		34,909	Mar 4	H Liverpool	1-1	Solskjaer 45	61,592
Oct 16	H Watford	4-1	Yorke 39, Cole 42 58, Irwin 44 (pen)	55,188	Mar 11	H Derby Co	3-1	Yorke 12, 70, 72	61,619
					Mar 16	A Leicester	2-0	Beckham 33, Yorke 83	22,170
					Mar 25	A Bradford	4-0	Yorke 37 46, Scholes 71, Beckham 79	18,276
Oct 23	A Tottenham	1-3	Giggs 23	36,072	Apr 1	H West Ham	7-1	Scholes 24 50 62, Irwin 26, Cole 45, Beckham 66, Solskjaer 73	61,611
Oct 30	H Aston Villa	3-0	Scholes 30, Cole 45, Keane 65	55,211					
Nov 6	H Leicester	2-0	Cole 30, 83	55,191	Apr 10	A Boro	4-3	Giggs 46, Cole 59, Scholes 74, Fortune 88	34,775
Nov 20	A Derby Co	2-1	Butt 53, Cole 83	33,378	Apr 15	H Sunderland	4-0	Solskjaer 2, 51, Butt 66, Berg 70	61,612
Dec 4	H Everton	5-1	Irwin 26 (pen), Solskjaer 29 43 52 58	55,133	Apr 22	A Southampton	3-1	Beckham 7, Benali og 15, Solskjaer 29	15,245
Dec 18	A West Ham	4-2	Yorke 9 62, Giggs 13 19	26,037					

THE RACE FOR NO.19

PAGE 42 THE MIRROR, Monday, April 16, 2001 mirrorsport@mgn.co.uk

MirrorSport tribute to the

FERGIE WILL NOT BE ABLE TO WALK AWAY

❛ He could go on winning trophies for years, and it's hard to give that up ❜

By JOHN CROSS and JAMES FLETCHER

ERIC CANTONA EXCLUSIVE

MANCHESTER United legend Eric Cantona last night claimed Sir Alex Ferguson may change his mind about retiring – because he is addicted to success.

Fergie has insisted he will leave the Old Trafford hot-seat at the end of next season after 15 years of unprecedented glory.

The championship is Fergie's 14th major honour with United and makes him the most successful manager in English football.

Desire

In total he has won seven championships, one European Cup, four FA Cups, one League Cup and one European Cup Winners' Cup.

And Cantona believes the 59-year-old United boss will find it almost impossible to walk away and give up the chance of winning more trophies.

Cantona, regarded as the catalyst for United's golden era of seven championships in nine years, is now an actor but would love to become United manager in the future.

Cantona said: "The secret of his success is desire. That's what drives him on and it's what he instils into every player.

"They must all have the desire to win trophies every season otherwise they will not survive at Old Trafford.

"That is what he looks for in every player he signs and he is the same. He never gets tired of winning things. He is a brilliant man.

"But that is why I think it will be the hardest decision to retire because he is the man who wants success the most.

"Sir Alex could go on winning trophies for years and it will be hard for him to give that up." That sheer hunger has not always made Ferguson popular, but he simply does not care.

His ruthless drive and insatiable desire have pushed United out of sight of their rivals.

That hunger has led him to study every single player more closely than any other manager to see whether they have what it takes to succeed at Old Trafford.

Steve Bruce, one-time defensive talisman at United and now manager of Second Division Wigan, said: "If you look at his squad and all of the stars in it, no one player is bigger than the club.

"Sir Alex is absolutely fantastic at getting the right blend of players who want success, who can fit into the dressing room, and who of course have great ability.

"They could be the best players in the world but if their attitude was wrong they wouldn't get a look-in at United because they have the potential to upset the dressing room. He always gets the perfect balance.

Drummed

"But I think the most important thing that he looks for in any player is desire and determination. He wants to know whether they have the same desire as him.

"That is why United are so successful and why they win trophies every season and why they have carried it on for years.

"I think the United squad love success and that is something drummed into them by Sir Alex from the very start."

Current stars Jaap Stam, Ryan Giggs and Dwight Yorke agree, insisting the club's success over the past decade is down to Ferguson and his determination to be the best.

Stam believes Ferguson is the best manager of all time – regardless of statistics.

He said: "He always puts the right teams on the pitch and he makes the right changes at crucial moments.

"He is not a manager who just buys for the sake of it, he looks carefully at the team and then decides what type of player he needs.

"Contrary to reports in the media, we're not scared of him. He's fair to all the players, although obviously if you're not straight with him you're not going to be the most happy person at Old Trafford.

"There's a lot of respect for him. Everybody knows what he's done for the club."

Giggs has been involved in all seven of United's Premiership successes and witnessed Ferguson's work first hand.

He believes the United manager is the best of all time and insists the players are driven by the prospect of rewarding him with more trophies.

Giggs said: "Alex Ferguson's drive is still as huge as it ever has been. His desire to keep on winning trophies is still there.

"You can see it when we only draw a game. He'll be upset that we haven't won."

And Dwight Yorke, who has fallen out with Ferguson during this campaign, added: "What can you say about Sir Alex?

"You have to give him credit because to win three championships on the trot just shows how much determination he has.

"He is a born winner and that spreads through to the players."

ERIC IDOL Cantona and Fergie were a dream team

NEVILLE: OUR ACHIEVEMENTS WON'T BE RECOGNISED FOR ANOTHER 20 YEARS

By JAMES FLETCHER

GARY NEVILLE believes Manchester United's success will not be fully appreciated for 20 years.

He claims their domestic dominance is taken for granted by too many people – including some at Old Trafford.

Neville feels that only after the fullness of time will Sir Alex Ferguson's achievements really be recognised. He said: "It is some achievement to win three in a row, though it won't probably be recognised for 15 to 20 years.

"At the moment, the way that everything is working, we are being judged on our European performances and the domestic championship seems to have been put on the back-burner. I think when people look back in 15 or 20 years they will realise that is quite a serious achievement.

"I suppose we have been victims of our own success on the domestic front.

"That's because we have won it by such a margin last year and this year and we lost the Charity Shield to Chelsea and people were saying they would challenge us, so would Leeds and Arsenal. Then all of a sudden we were 15 or 16 points clear and it didn't become so important.

"But it is the most important thing. Maybe even the memory of losing the championship is fading from United as well.

"I know that is serious devastation for us, losing the domestic championship. It is our bread and butter no matter what people think."

manager who made history

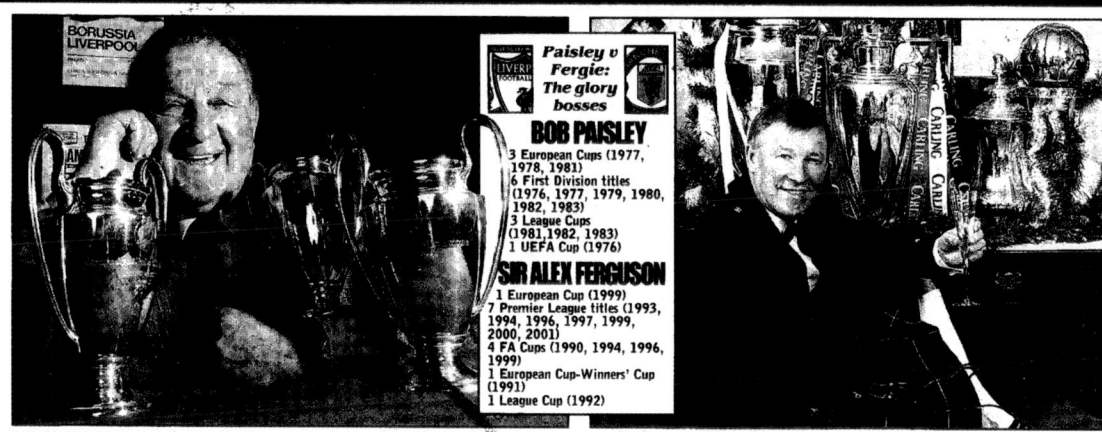

Paisley v Fergie: The glory bosses

BOB PAISLEY
3 European Cups (1977, 1978, 1981)
6 First Division titles (1976, 1977, 1979, 1980, 1982, 1983)
3 League Cups (1981, 1982, 1983)
1 UEFA Cup (1976)

SIR ALEX FERGUSON
1 European Cup (1999)
7 Premier League titles (1993, 1994, 1996, 1997, 1999, 2000, 2001)
4 FA Cups (1990, 1994, 1996, 1999)
1 European Cup-Winners' Cup (1991)
1 League Cup (1992)

SIX OF THE BEST: Bob Paisley led Liverpool to half a dozen league championships

SIMPLY THE BEST: Ferguson has proved himself the greatest manager ever

Yes Sir Alex, you are even better than my old boss Bob Paisley
Mark Lawrenson
FOOTBALL'S No.1 EXPERT

SIR ALEX Ferguson has not only eclipsed Bob Paisley by winning seven Premiership titles – he also confirmed himself as the greatest manager in English football history.

It is very difficult to compare bosses from different eras, but for me it is much harder to manage now than when Paisley led Liverpool to six league championships.

I was lucky enough to be part of Paisley's golden era at Anfield when Liverpool dominated English football in the late 1970s and early 80s in the same way Manchester United are now doing.

But the biggest difference Fergie faces and what sets him apart from Paisley and the rest is: How on earth do you motivate millionaires?

United stars like Roy Keane, David Beckham and Jaap Stam have all been there, seen it and are already so rich they will never have to work again after they hang up their boots.

So for Fergie to drive them to success after success, trophy after trophy, season after season makes it a truly remarkable achievement which sets them apart from what Paisley achieved.

Don't get me wrong, I'm not in any way belittling Paisley's achievements, but Fergie deserves the highest praise possible for putting United on a different planet.

Both managers effectively built great teams – and then went out and assembled another. Paisley did it to great effect and Fergie was blessed with a second coming when Butt, Beckham, Scholes and the two Nevilles worked their way through the ranks.

United have a great blend of foreign flair, Northern grit and a love of proving people wrong – just as they might do in Munich on Wednesday.

Those five help make up the core of the best team in the Premiership and the amazing thing is they are all in their mid-20s with their best years to come.

Fergie will retire at the end of next season so you can bet next year he will want to win absolutely everything going.

And, worryingly for the likes of Arsenal, Leeds and Liverpool, while I can see them getting closer to United, I can't see anyone toppling them.

United have this great knack which no other team in the Premiership has of being able to play poorly and still win. That is their biggest single quality.

While Ferguson will be an impossible act to follow, he will leave a great legacy for whoever comes in, whether it be Steve McClaren or a big-name foreign coach.

The only team I can see emerging is Leeds, whose youngsters and their determination remind me of United in their early stages of development.

I know Fergie disagrees with me on this, and it in no way devalues his achievement, but United have not had to be anywhere near their best this season.

The simple truth is no one has pushed them and the Premiership has been mediocre. It's a damning indictment on the rest, but United have won before Easter, at a canter and with no real competition.

People keep saying Teddy Sheringham will be their player of the year but for me it should be Roy Keane, the real driving force on the pitch.

But just when the rest think they will be able to offer a better challenge for the title next season, I am convinced Fergie will go out and buy big this summer and get the likes of Ruud Van Nistelrooy and a world class midfielder.

That is what keeps them ahead of the rest.

It's an age-old recipe for success to keep everyone on their toes in the dressing room. Fergie has been a master at it.

Paisley did it with us at Anfield. He went and bought Gary Gillespie when Alan Hansen and I were at our peak. We looked at each other and said: "What on earth has he done that for?" But it pushed us on another level.

Fergie gets the best out of his players.

Paisley was the nice guy who gave you tremendous self-belief and relied on Joe Fagan and Ronnie Moran to put a bomb under the players.

Paisley would instil great confidence. He would say to me and Hansen: "Have you played against these strikers before?" We would nod and he'd just say: "Well, I'll leave it up to you."

That gives players such confidence, knowing the manager has 100 per cent trust in their ability.

Fergie does everything, giving out the rollickings and the praise, and there is very little he needs to delegate to Steve McClaren.

That brings me to whether United's best XI could beat Paisley's first choice team.

It's an extremely difficult question to answer.

They were similar in that both teams used a 4-4-2 system but even with the aid of modern science, I wouldn't like to predict who would come out on top if they played each other ten times.

This United team with Beckham, Giggs, Keane and Scholes would probably just have the edge in midfield.

But our Liverpool team had Kenny Dalglish and Ian Rush which, for me, is a better strike partnership than anything United could offer.

It's just too close to call, but then I would say that.

Interview: JOHN CROSS

Is Mark right? Fax us on 020 7293 3739 or e-mail: mirrorsport@mgn.co.uk

Lawro's best Liverpool and United line-ups

LIVERPOOL	MAN UTD
Grobbelaar	Barthez
Neal	G.Neville
Hansen	Stam
Lawrenson	Brown
Nicol	Irwin
Lee	Beckham
McDermott	Keane
Souness	Scholes
Whelan	Giggs
Dalglish	Sheringham
Rush	Cole

CROWDED OUT: A full house cheers United's 1999 title, but Old Trafford was empty this time round

TV RUINED TITLE PARTY
FROM BACK PAGE
into Asia and America could ultimately lead to even more erratic kick-off times.

"If EastEnders can hold sway over the UEFA Cup who is to say we will not be kicking off matches in the middle of the night to suit fans in Asia," added Houston.

"The timings of games are not suited for the fans who actually travel to watch the matches. The day Blackburn won the title they had the United game and Blackburn game both on at the same time, with split screen. But this year everyone pretty much expected that United would win it.

"It shows the disjointed nature of football in modern times. Now it is all about suiting the broadcaster, not the fans."

A Sky spokesman said: "The race is hard to predict. United's televised game gave them the critical points but Arsenal's surprise home defeat decided the title."

SALUTE: McClaren

McCLAREN HAILS HIS HEROES
By JAMES FLETCHER

STEVE McCLAREN last night paid tribute to Manchester United's record-breaking players.

He insists their seventh Premiership title was a result of their incredible levels of consistency.

McClaren claims the Old Trafford squad are driven on by their domestic success – though he does not believe next season will be so easy.

He said: "Our success has got to amount to consistency – our away performances prove that.

"To win the championship you need to perform away from home, and apart from Leeds, we are the only ones who have done that well.

Amazed

"It comes down to the durability and resilience of the players, which they have shown over the years.

"They just keep on going. They grind out results even when they are below par. It is all about character."

McClaren was amazed by the spirit of United's squad when he first arrived from Derby, but believes their Premiership dominance may ultimately have hurt them in Europe.

He added: "Our big lead in the league could be the reason why we have spluttered a bit in Europe. You have to learn to keep up your standards throughout the year.

"But most definitely it will be harder next season. Leeds have shown in the second half of the season how good they can be and all our main rivals are gaining experience in Europe."

NOW MAKE IT FOUR ME
FROM BACK PAGE

for English football to see those three clubs doing so well in Europe this season.

"There is so much potential for a terrific championship next time."

In recognition of this season's successful campaign, Carling will recommend to the Premier League that Old Trafford would be a fitting home for the original silver trophy.

A Carling spokesman said last night: "We shall be talking to the Premier League about the destiny of the trophy. Most certainly one of the possibilities would be to give it to United.

"The decision will be a joint one but we feel it would be a most proper acknowledgment of Manchester United's and Sir Alex Ferguson's awesome record during our sponsorship."

THE RACE FOR NO.19

DAILY Mirror
Monday May 5 2003

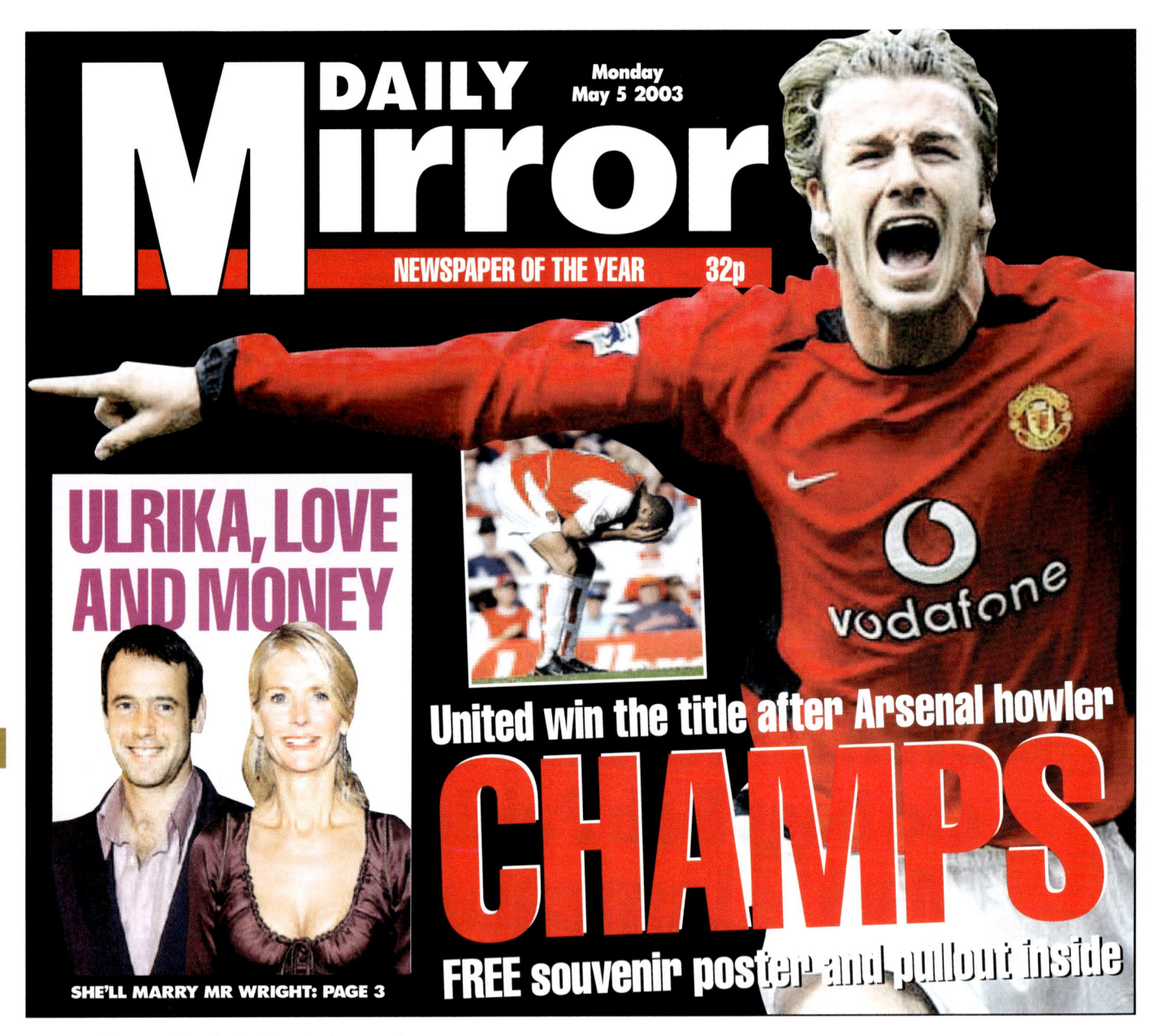

NEWSPAPER OF THE YEAR 32p

ULRIKA, LOVE AND MONEY

SHE'LL MARRY MR WRIGHT: PAGE 3

United win the title after Arsenal howler

CHAMPS

FREE souvenir poster and pullout inside

Beck at the top: The Daily Mirror's front and back pages announce the 2002/03 title success after United came from behind to pip Arsenal

FINAL TABLE 2000/01

		Pld	W	D	L	F	A	GD	Pts
1	Manchester United	38	24	8	6	79	31	48	80
2	Arsenal	38	20	10	8	63	38	25	70
3	Liverpool	38	20	9	9	71	39	32	69
4	Leeds United	38	20	8	10	64	43	21	68
5	Ipswich Town	38	20	6	12	57	42	15	66
6	Chelsea	38	17	10	11	68	45	23	61
7	Sunderland	38	15	12	11	46	41	5	57
8	Aston Villa	38	13	15	10	46	43	3	54
9	Charlton Athletic	38	14	10	14	50	57	-7	52
10	Southampton	38	14	10	14	40	48	-8	52
11	Newcastle United	38	14	9	15	44	50	-6	51
12	Tottenham Hotspur	38	13	10	15	47	54	-7	49
13	Leicester City	38	14	6	18	39	51	-12	48
14	Middlesbrough	38	9	15	14	44	44	0	42
15	West Ham United	38	10	12	16	45	50	-5	42
16	Everton	38	11	9	18	45	59	-14	42
17	Derby County	38	10	12	16	37	59	-22	42
18	Manchester City	38	8	10	20	41	65	-24	34
19	Coventry City	38	8	10	20	36	63	-27	34
20	Bradford City	38	5	11	22	30	70	-40	26

FINAL TABLE 2002/03

		Pld	W	D	L	F	A	GD	Pts
1	Manchester United	38	25	8	5	74	34	40	83
2	Arsenal	38	23	9	6	85	42	43	78
3	Newcastle United	38	21	6	11	63	48	15	69
4	Chelsea	38	19	10	9	68	38	30	67
5	Liverpool	38	18	10	10	61	41	20	64
6	Blackburn Rovers	38	16	12	10	52	43	9	60
7	Everton	38	17	8	13	48	49	-1	59
8	Southampton	38	13	13	12	43	46	-3	52
9	Manchester City	38	15	6	17	47	54	-7	51
10	Tottenham Hotspur	38	14	8	16	51	62	-11	50
11	Middlesbrough	38	13	10	15	48	44	4	49
12	Charlton Athletic	38	14	7	17	45	56	-11	49
13	Birmingham City	38	13	9	16	41	49	-8	48
14	Fulham	38	13	9	16	41	50	-9	48
15	Leeds United	38	14	5	19	58	57	1	47
16	Aston Villa	38	12	9	17	42	47	-5	45
17	Bolton Wanderers	38	10	14	14	41	51	-10	44
18	West Ham United	38	10	12	16	42	59	-17	42
19	West Bromwich Albion	38	6	8	24	29	65	-36	26
20	Sunderland	38	4	7	27	21	65	-44	19

MirrorSport
mirrorsport@mgn.co.uk

ON DAY UNITED WON THE CHAMPIONSHIP

INSIDE: UNITED TITLE SPECIAL PULL-OUT

WINNER

Fergie: This is the sweetest title yet

By DAVID McDONNELL

SIR ALEX FERGUSON last night hailed his Manchester United "heroes" for their dramatic Premiership triumph over Arsenal – then challenged his players to recapture the European Cup.

Arsenal's 3-2 defeat to Leeds at Highbury handed United their eighth Premiership title in 11 years.

But amid all the euphoria of United's triumph, Fergie focused his attention on the next challenge and said: "This is our greatest achievement but now we have to get the big one again. By that I mean the European Cup.

"Winning it twice is not enough for a club of this size.

"We're not far away, believe me. We want it again and going out to Real Madrid has only made us more determined to be European champions again."

United's Premiership triumph confirmed Ferguson as officially the greatest British manager of all-time, with 27 trophies in 29 years of

TURN TO PAGE 43

TOP OF PREMIERSHIP

	P	W	D	L	F	A	Pts
Man Utd	37	24	8	5	72	33	80
Arsenal	36	21	9	6	75	41	72
Newcastle	37	21	5	11	61	46	68
Chelsea	37	18	10	9	66	37	64
Liverpool	37	18	10	9	60	39	64
Everton	37	17	8	12	47	47	59

BUBBLING OVER: Sir Alex Ferguson after Manchester United clinched the League title yesterday

Picture courtesy of manutdpics.com

..and a very sore loser

HE DAREN'T LOOK: Arsene Wenger's gloom

By JOHN CROSS
Arsenal 2 Leeds Utd 3

ARSENE Wenger last night insisted Arsenal are still a better team than Manchester United – even after throwing away the Premiership title at Highbury yesterday.

Sir Alex Ferguson's United heroes clinched their eighth championship in 11 years after Arsenal crashed to a shock home defeat which ensured Leeds' Premiership survival.

But Arsenal boss Wenger claimed United only won the title because Arsenal tossed it away. He said: "I'm bitterly disappointed. When you

TURN TO PAGE 41

"In football there are some guys that you just know something is going to happen when they're on the ball. There are players who are good, who can do some nice things with the ball but there are special players. Ronaldo is definitely one of them. He's a strong lad who has a bit of everything. There are very few players who have all those attributes. Maradona had it and Ronaldo has it too"

– Denis Law

MirrorSport

Chelsea bow out like champions

INSIDE: MANIA SPECIAL ON DAY THE TITLE WENT BACK TO OLD TRAFFORD

JOSE TAKES IT ON THE CHIN

MY BRAVES: Jose Mourinho hugs skipper John Terry (left) and Frank Lampard after their draw yesterday

CHAMPIONSHIP: THE FINAL DAY

Burnley......1 Coventry...2	Luton......0 Sunderland 5
Colchester 0 C.Palace... 2	Preston ...1 Birm'gham 0
Derby........2 Leeds Utd 0	QPR.........1 Stoke City.. 1
Hull City.... 1 Plymouth 2	Sheff Wed 3 Norwich...... 2
Ipswich......3 Cardiff......1	South'pton 4 Southend... 1
Leicester... 1 Wolves..... 4	West Brom 7 Barnsley.... 0

KING KEANO: SUNDERLAND GO UP AS CHAMPIONS MANIA PAGES 12 & 13

I DID IT MY WAY

Fergie: My title winners are just fantastic..and I am carrying on

By DAVID ANDERSON

SIR ALEX FERGUSON last night celebrated his ninth and greatest title success – then revealed he is ready to carry on for at least another two years.

The Manchester United boss feels he has answered critics who questioned his ability following three seasons without lifting the Premiership trophy.

After Chelsea's draw at Arsenal yesterday handed the crown to United, Fergie said: "I think winning the title at any time is great, but this is a new team and they've done fantastic.

"I can't speak more highly of them than I could of any other players in the world.

"There was unfair criticism of the players because it was a changing team and my role as manager is to make some terrible decisions sometimes and more on lads who have been terrific servants to this club because we have to change.

"Age catches up with a lot of them, like it did with Roy Keane, and with young

TURN TO PAGE 51

LOVELY BUBBLY: Fergie gets ready to toast winning the Premiership

---

ROEDER OUT, SAM IN

NEW ROED: Roeder's set to be replaced by Allardyce (right)

By SIMON BIRD

GLENN Roeder quit as Newcastle boss last night on a £1million pay-off, with Sam Allardyce willing to accept the Newcastle hot-seat at the end of the season. Bookies have stopped taking bets on Allardyce's arrival, though the deal is not yet sealed and there are complications. Now the United job is vacant other candidates could emerge, including Blackburn boss Mark Hughes and UEFA Cup and La Liga championship challenging Sevilla boss Juande Ramos. Chairman Freddy Shepherd held emergency meetings at St James' Park yesterday in a no-holds-barred inquest into another failed season. Roeder agreed to resign and to walk away with a year's salary in a clean break with the north-east club.

Newcastle are now

TURN TO PAGE 47

THE RACE FOR NO.19

PAGE 48 **DAILY MIRROR**, Monday, May 7, 2007 mirrorsport@mgn.co.uk

UNITED CHAMPIONS! FERGIE WIN

I CAN'T LOOK: Wayne Rooney turns away.. and doesn't see Edwin van der Sar save Darius Vassell's penalty

SIR ALEX HAILS BRAVEHEARTS
Players bounce back from Euro low

**Man City 0
Man Utd 1**

By DAVID ANDERSON

To win the Premiership you need great ability, luck, and bucketloads of character.

At Bolton, Manchester United showed their class; at Anfield their good fortune; and at Manchester City on Saturday their strength of character.

After being humiliated in Europe, and after spending an hour sitting on the tarmac at Milan airport in the early hours of Thursday morning, United could have done manager. "To come back from Wednesday's disappointment and have the 12.45 kick-off wasn't easy.

"But we saw it through and that showed real courage. Every one of those players deserves credit for that."

Rio Ferdinand, who made a successful return from his groin injury, was also proud of the way United bounced and bouncing back to win a league game. We've done it again here and that's the sign of a team that wins things."

At key moments during United's title campaign, different players have stepped up to the plate and proved their mettle and against City it was Edwin van der Sar and that man Ronaldo again.

Mettle

Ronaldo exacted his revenge on the thuggish Ball when he drew him into fouling him for

Beauty
HOW FREE-FLOWING UNITED

Martin Lipton
CHIEF FOOTBALL WRITER

A NINTH title and Sir Alex Ferguson's greatest triumph – in the season that showed footballing beauty can conquer the relentless beast.

Fergie's warm relationship with Jose Mourinho has gone into the deep freeze in recent weeks, the tense nature of the contest seeing both men making statements they may come to regret.

But while the Laird of Old Trafford was on the golf course yesterday as Chelsea finally gave up the ghost, nothing should diminish the joy of this title victory, the final proof that Ferguson can build team after team.

Pleasure

Yes, United's Treble ambitions were swept away amid the torrents which fell on the San Siro last Wednesday, befuddled and bewitched by the genius of Kaka.

But no team has given greater pleasure, has captivated the nation, has played with a spirit of adventure and entertainment more than United this term.

Think of Paul Scholes, back to his buzzing, tempo-setting best, capable of playing sublime passes in spaces so tight merely finding a team-mate is a feat.

Look at the development of Michael Carrick, who might have been weighed down by that £18million price-tag, but who has instead prospered and grown, becoming the midfield conductor he always threatened to be.

Delight, once more, in Ryan Giggs. No longer the will o' the wisp of his youth yet still able to ghost into spaces, show his marker a clean pair of heels, and drive home his side's superiority.

Be thankful for the talent of Wayne Rooney, showing strength anew to bring himself out of a slump in form and confidence that appeared as if it might consume him, but who came good when his side needed him most.

And most importantly of all, hail the majesty of the new king, Cristiano Ronaldo, who began the season as the country's whipping boy and ended it as the manifestation of why United deserve their crown.

But while the players deserve their accolades, what about the man who put them together, who infused them with his own spirit?

As Mourinho the arch-pragmatist and his win-at-all-costs attitude led the Chelsea hunt for a third straight title it needed something special to deny them. And Fergie, as so often before, provided that, carried his belief that there was glory in playing the right way.

Yes, he has been here before. Ending that 26-year wait to claim the first Premiership in 1993 was a huge achievement, and the wins that followed as he built and rebuilt sides to take on first Blackburn's millions, then the passion of Newcastle and ultimately the shrewd footballing artistry

TAKE IT AS RED: United players show their delight after taking three points in the derby clash with Man City and virtually sealing the title

FERGIE'S NINE TITLES
1992-93 Runners-up: Aston Villa
1993-94 Runners-up: Blackburn
1995-96 Runners-up: Newcastle
1996-97 Runners-up: Newcastle
1998-99 Runners-up: Arsenal
1999-2000 Runners-up: Arsenal
2000-01 Runners-up: Arsenal
2002-03 Runners-up: Arsenal
2006-07 Runners-up: Chelsea

FINAL TABLE 2006/07

		Pld	W	D	L	F	A	GD	Pts
1	Manchester United	38	28	5	5	83	27	56	89
2	Chelsea	38	24	11	3	64	24	40	83
3	Liverpool	38	20	8	10	57	27	30	68
4	Arsenal	38	19	11	8	63	35	28	68
5	Tottenham Hotspur	38	17	9	12	57	54	3	60
6	Everton	38	15	13	10	52	36	16	58
7	Bolton Wanderers	38	16	8	14	47	52	-5	56
8	Reading	38	16	7	15	52	47	5	55
9	Portsmouth	38	14	12	12	45	42	3	54
10	Blackburn Rovers	38	15	7	16	52	54	-2	52
11	Aston Villa	38	11	17	10	43	41	2	50
12	Middlesbrough	38	12	10	16	44	49	-5	46
13	Newcastle United	38	11	10	17	38	47	-9	43
14	Manchester City	38	11	9	18	29	44	-15	42
15	West Ham United	38	12	5	21	35	59	-24	41
16	Fulham	38	8	15	15	38	60	-22	39
17	Wigan Athletic	38	10	8	20	37	59	-22	38
18	Sheffield United	38	10	8	20	32	55	-23	38
19	Charlton Athletic	38	8	10	20	34	60	-26	34
20	Watford	38	5	13	20	29	59	-30	28

HOW THE CHAMPIONS RATED

Mirror Chief Football Writer MARTIN LIPTON assesses the contribution of the 23 major players in Sir Alex Ferguson's brilliant recapture of the Barclays Premiership title..

EDWIN VAN DER SAR
31 starts, 12 clean sheets
The big Dutchman made a few blunders but they were more than compensated for by his series of key saves in the biggest games. Brought confidence to the back four and made United look solid again.
SEASON RATING: 8

GARY NEVILLE
24 starts, no goals
Injury-hit this season but still the barrack-room lawyer and organiser in chief at the back. His experience and consistency is a benchmark for his eventual successor to live up to. Nobody will enjoy this title more than the skipper.
SEASON RATING: 7

RIO FERDINAND
33 starts, 1 goal
The odd wobble and at times needed the comforting presence of Vidic alongside him. Sometimes it is too easy for Rio but his absence was a key factor in United's Champions League exit.
SEASON RATING: 7

HIS 9TH (AND GREATEST) TITLE

killed the beast

PROVED JUST TOO MUCH FOR BRUTE FORCE OF BLUES

BARCLAYS PREMIERSHIP

mirrorsport@mgn.co.uk DAILY MIRROR, Monday, May 7, 2007 PAGE 49

WIN tickets to Chelsea v Man Utd!

IT IS the match Chelsea will be determined not to lose on Wednesday and you can be there when Jose Mourinho's men play newly-crowned Premiership champions Manchester United.

Mirror Sport have teamed up with Samsung, official sponsors of Chelsea, to offer you the chance to win a pair of tickets to see the Blues in action against Fergie's double chasers.

And that's not all! The lucky winner will also receive a state-of-the-art Samsung K5 MP3 Player featuring a 1.7 inch display screen, built-in speakers, 30 hours' playback, an FM radio receiver and an alarm clock.

Just phone the number below and answer the following question:

0901 609 2320

Q: Who did Manchester United wrestle the Premiership title from yesterday?

Normal Mirror Sport rules apply. The Sports Editor's decision is final. Calls cost 60p per minute and will last no longer than two minutes. Lines close at 6pm today (Monday).

For the full range of Samsung products including mobile phones and home entertainment systems visit HYPERLINK "http://www.samsung.co.uk" www.samsung.co.uk

---

of Arsene Wenger's Arsenal were evidence of Ferguson's unique talent. But the landscape changed when Roman Abramovich bought Chelsea, altering United's unchallenged economic dominance and seemingly taking its toll on Ferguson too.

After Wenger's 'Invincibles' ground United down in 2004, the arrival of Mourinho added the necessary organisation, discipline and purpose to Abramovich's unprecedented expenditure and even Fergie could do nothing to prevent the 'Special One' sweeping all before him. Over two seasons United were 30 points behind the Blues, the departure of Roy Keane seemingly signalling the end of an era as Ferguson's reign appeared destined to end in failure, his authority and drive ebbing away.

Emotional

Nobody can say that now. His team sent out a message of intent with their 5-1 thumping of Fulham in their opening game and they simply kept on playing. While Mourinho was fighting with his board in the January transfer window, Ferguson pulled off a masterstroke by bringing in Henrik Larsson on a short-term loan, the Swede galvanising Old Trafford with his perception and movement.

But this time they did not have to see off a Newcastle side exposed by Kevin Keegan's soft emotional shell, or even an Arsenal side who can be bullied off the park.

This was Chelsea, the voracious Blue machine, the bulldozer that keeps on coming, fuelled by the mercurial presence of Mourinho. Yet when it mattered, United found the key moments at the vital times.

Ronaldo at Fulham, skipping down the left to win a game that should have been lost. John O'Shea in front of The Kop a week later, an act of larceny that struck deep into Chelsea guts.

And then, as they looked to be giving everything away last weekend, two down at Everton while Chelsea led Bolton, the great surge, sheer desire – and the ability to capitalise on one mistake by poor Iain Turner – turning things around in the space of half an hour, to leave Fergie doing his 'granddad dance' on the sidelines.

Bitter

Maybe he should leave the routine to those with just one left foot.

But the enthusiasm and excitement, burning from the eyes that have seen so much in football, showed beyond doubt that this really mattered, that Ferguson realised the nature of the peak he and his team were poised to conquer.

The only shame is that it was won in anti-climax, not by United's Ronaldo-inspired win over bitter rivals City at Eastlands, but by Wenger putting the final nail in Mourinho's championship coffin at the Emirates.

But let there be no doubt, Ferguson and United are back where they deserve to be.

The best team, the best football. Simply the best.

Mirror Sport guide to the men who brought title back to Old Trafford

NEMANJA VIDIC
24 starts, 3 goals
The new Steve Bruce, and a big factor this season. Dominant in the air at both ends, gave United the reassurance that was missing for the last two seasons. Came back too early in Milan but a towering influence.
SEASON RATING: 9

PATRICE EVRA
21 starts, 2 subs, 1 goal
Took advantage of Heinze's early-season injuries to become first choice and looked the real thing as he came to terms with English football. Positional sense good and gave zest coming forward.
SEASON RATING: 7

CRISTIANO RONALDO
32 starts, 1 sub, 17 goals
Unplayable all season and simply magnificent. Could have walked away after the World Cup but instead set about showing his true worth. Getting him to agree a new deal is Fergie's best signing since Cantona.
SEASON RATING: 10

MICHAEL CARRICK
28 starts, 3 subs, 3 goals
Old Trafford has broken many players in the past but Carrick has thrived on the responsibility and the challenge to establish himself as a genuine United player. Nobody can doubt him for leaving Spurs now.
SEASON RATING: 8

PAUL SCHOLES
29 starts, 6 goals
Past his prime? Who are you kidding? Has replaced Roy Keane as the heartbeat of the team, retaining all the instincts that made him a revelation but adding the extra knowledge gained through experience. Terrific.
SEASON RATING: 9

RYAN GIGGS
25 starts, 4 subs, 4 goals
The former boy wonder has evolved into Mr Versatile, equally adept out wide, in the engine room or running free through the middle. Still has the keys to unlock defences and has a few more years left.
SEASON RATING: 8

WAYNE ROONEY
32 starts, 1 sub, 14 goals
Down in the dumps in the autumn, back at the summit when it mattered after the arrival of Henrik Larsson brought a spring to his step. Ends the campaign with a big smile and his first championship medal.
SEASON RATING: 8

HENRIK LARSSON
5 starts, one sub, 1 goal
The statistics say he was a bit-part player but the truth is very different. Larsson energised Old Trafford and brought a new dynamic to the team. The signing of the season.
SEASON RATING: 8

CONTINUED ON PAGES 50 & 51

THE RACE FOR NO.19

58 M SPORT
Daily Mirror MONDAY 12.05.2008

BARCLAYS PREMIER LEAGUE

IT'S FERGIE'S TITLE AGAIN! WIGAN 0 MANCHEST

AWESOME TW

New sensation Ronaldo and old master Giggs are the title-winning heroes

COMPUTER
WIGAN
MANCHESTER UNITED
UNITED BOSS IT ON GLORY DAY

BALL POSSESSION
37%
63%

FACE TO FACE
5 Corners 12
2 Offside 0
69% Pass completion 82%
27 Tackles 28
10 Fouls 6
3 Cards 2

SHOTS
7 off target 5
4 on target 6

MAN OF THE MATCH
Ryan Giggs (MAN UTD)
7 Record number of United appearances

VILLAIN OF THE MATCH
Emmerson Boyce (WIGAN)
5 His clumsy challenge gave United a penalty

ANORAK
Ryan Giggs' goal was his first away from Old Trafford since October last year

1-0 Cristiano Ronaldo makes no mistake from the penalty spot to put United in front at Wigan yesterday

BY DAVID McDONNELL
d.mcdonnell@mirror.co.uk

THERE could not have been two more fitting goalscorers for Manchester United as Sir Alex Ferguson's side clinched a 10th Premier League crown.

Cristiano Ronaldo and Ryan Giggs are at opposite ends of their United careers, but both epitomise the unique character and desire required to succeed at the world's team mates as the perfect script unfolded.

His place in United history is already secure, a 10th championship medal adding another chapter to Giggs's remarkable Old Trafford story. And he will write another in the Champions League Final in Moscow on May 21 when he will make Charlton's record his own.

United rarely sparkled but this win was all about character and spirit, embodied by their remarkable boss.

Fergie scoffed at suggestions he may retire if United win the European Cup.

22nd minute when Rio Ferdinand stuck out an arm to divert a goal-bound shot from Jason Koumas. Replays seemed to confirm Ferdinand's intent.

Wigan's anger was compounded in the 32nd minute when referee Steve Bennett handed United a spot-kick following a clumsy trip on Wayne Rooney from Emmerson Boyce.

Ronaldo, who had missed the last time he had taken a penalty in the first leg of United's Champions League semi final in the Nou Camp, sent Chris Kirkland the wrong way for his

reduced to 10 men, the outcome could have been very different.

While their lead remained so slender and with Chelsea offering no let up with their dogged pursuit, one goal from Wigan would have wrenched the title from United's grasp.

And it very nearly came in the 69th minute when Emile Heskey headed just over the bar.

But with 10 minutes to go, Giggs secured the title, sweeping the ball into the net with his famed left foot. For a split second he could not quite believe it, his expression one

---

56 M SPORT
Daily Mirror MONDAY 12.05.2008

Football Spy
THE GAME'S ORIGINAL GOSSIP COLUMN.. THE HOTTEST NEWS..EVERY SINGLE DAY

SPURS IN FIGHT TO NET SAM
COME 'EAR Eto'o is wanted

By TOM COLLOMOSSE

TOTTENHAM could be pipped by Inter Milan to the signing of Samuel Eto'o after the Italians launched a £32million bid to land the striker.

Spurs have turned to Eto'o, 27, after admitting defeat in their quest to keep Dimitar Berbatov at White Hart Lane.

But boss Juande Ramos may struggle to see off the threat from Inter, especially as the Serie A club can offer Champions League football next season.

Inter reckon Eto'o - who

has 47 caps for Cameroon - will form a deadly partnership with Zlatan Ibrahimovic as chairman Massimo Moratti eyes an all-out assault on the European crown.

DUTCH coach Aad De Mos has set his sights on the West Ham job.

The former Ajax, PSV Eindhoven and Werder Bremen manager, who left Vitesse Arnhem two weeks, said: "It's a club I'd love the chance to manage one day.

"If an opportunity ever arose it would be very difficult to turn down."

WEST BROM DEFENDER PAUL ROBINSON COULD ROCK THE BAGGIES' PROMOTION PARTY BY JOINING CELTIC THIS SUMMER

BRUCE CHASING BIG GREEK STAR | **KEANE EYES UP FOLEY SWOOP**

WIGAN boss Steve Bruce is ready to make a £4million move for one of the biggest names in the | SUNDERLAND are ready to bid £2.5m for Wolves right-back Kevin Foley (above). Republic Of Ireland inter

---

IT'S SIR ALEX'S TITLE AGAIN   WIGAN 0 MA

PERFECT TE

Fergie picks up 10th Premier League cro reveals secret of his success: his wife C

1993 1994 1996 1997 1999 2000 2001 2003

Left and below: A tenth title in 16 seasons was just the start of the celebrations as a third European Cup would be won 10 days later. Overleaf, three in a row takes United's championship tally to 18

FINAL TABLE 2007/08

		Pld	W	D	L	F	A	GD	Pts
1	Manchester United	38	27	6	5	80	22	58	87
2	Chelsea	38	25	10	3	65	26	39	85
3	Arsenal	38	24	11	3	74	31	43	83
4	Liverpool	38	21	13	4	67	28	39	76
5	Everton	38	19	8	11	55	33	22	65
6	Aston Villa	38	16	12	10	71	51	20	60
7	Blackburn Rovers	38	15	13	10	50	48	2	58
8	Portsmouth	38	16	9	13	48	40	8	57
9	Manchester City	38	15	10	13	45	53	-8	55
10	West Ham United	38	13	10	15	42	50	-8	49
11	Tottenham Hotspur	38	11	13	14	66	61	5	46
12	Newcastle United	38	11	10	17	45	65	-20	43
13	Middlesbrough	38	10	12	16	43	53	-10	42
14	Wigan Athletic	38	10	10	18	34	51	-17	40
15	Sunderland	38	11	6	21	36	59	-23	39
16	Bolton Wanderers	38	9	10	19	36	54	-18	37
17	Fulham	38	8	12	18	38	60	-22	36
18	Reading	38	10	6	22	41	66	-25	36
19	Birmingham City	38	8	11	19	46	62	-16	35
20	Derby County	38	1	8	29	20	89	-69	11

FINAL TABLE 2008/09

		Pld	W	D	L	F	A	GD	Pts
1	Manchester United	38	28	6	4	68	24	44	90
2	Liverpool	38	25	11	2	77	27	50	86
3	Chelsea	38	25	8	5	68	24	44	83
4	Arsenal	38	20	12	6	68	37	31	72
5	Everton	38	17	12	9	55	37	18	63
6	Aston Villa	38	17	11	10	54	48	6	62
7	Fulham	38	14	11	13	39	34	5	53
8	Tottenham Hotspur	38	14	9	15	45	45	0	51
9	West Ham United	38	14	9	15	42	45	-3	51
10	Manchester City	38	15	5	18	58	50	8	50
11	Wigan Athletic	38	12	9	17	34	45	-11	45
12	Stoke City	38	12	9	17	38	55	-17	45
13	Bolton Wanderers	38	11	8	19	41	53	-12	41
14	Portsmouth	38	10	11	17	38	57	-19	41
15	Blackburn Rovers	38	10	11	17	40	60	-20	41
16	Sunderland	38	9	9	20	34	54	-20	36
17	Hull City	38	8	11	19	39	64	-25	35
18	Newcastle United	38	7	13	18	40	59	-19	34
19	Middlesbrough	38	7	11	20	28	57	-29	32
20	West Bromwich Albion	38	8	8	22	36	67	-31	32

When FOOTBALL Was FOOTBALL

MANCHESTER UNITED
A Nostalgic Look at a Century of the Club

OUT NOW £18.99 plus P&P
Call 01963 442030 & quote WF.

This is a unique and magnificent collection of photographs of Manchester United from its early days until 1992.

www.MirrorFootball.co.uk
Available from all good bookshops or
ORDER DIRECT on Tel: 01963 442030

Books for enthusiasts by enthusiasts

Haynes

Daily Mirror, May 18, Season 08-09

Mania

UNITED SPECIAL
CHAMPIONS 2008-2009

THE 18 TITLES ...AND GIGGS HAS HELPED WIN 11 OF 'EM
FIRST DIVISION
1908, 1911, 1952, 1956, 1957, 1965, 1967
PREMIER LEAGUE
1993, 1994, 1996, 1997, 1999, 2000, 2001, 2003, 2007, 2008, 2009

Another season, another crown for Sir Alex who roars: Now make it 19

By DAVID McDONNELL

SIR ALEX FERGUSON has set his sights on a record 19th title for Manchester United.

After the draw with Arsenal which made it league crown No.18 – equalling Liverpool's total – the United boss said: "Next year we want to go for it again. Never in a million years did I think we could get on terms with Liverpool. What will make it even more special is when we get in front of them."

Ryan Giggs pocketed his 11th league winners' medal, then hailed United's latest success one of the most satisfying.

"You never get used to winning titles," said Giggs. "It still gives you the same buzz. This one was extra special because we did it at Old Trafford in front of our fans, which we've only done once before.

"Liverpool were really strong all season and pushed us right to the end, so I'm sure they'll be back next year. Over the last five or six years it's definitely got tougher to win."

UNITED GAME BY GAME: 2&3

KING FERGIE

THE RACE FOR NO 19

"Ryan [Giggs] has got everything. He could turn into one of the greatest ever"

– George Best, speaking in 1993

Gary Pallister

"I'D just joined Manchester United. I was living in a hotel, there was very little to do, and I went to see an FA Youth Cup match at Old Trafford. Paul Ince and I sat in the directors' box with Alex Ferguson and he said: 'There's a kid playing tonight who's going to be special.' Ryan was still at school, I think he was 15, and we saw this spindly little pipe cleaner of a footballer running amok on the left-hand side. You could see straight off that he had a special gift."

Carlos Quieroz

"HE is one of those special and rare players who could play football in a phone box and would always find the door no matter how many players you put in there with him."

Eric Cantona, speaking in 2001

"THE secret of his success is desire. That's what drives him on and it's what he instils into every player.

They must all have the desire to win trophies every season otherwise they will not survive at Old Trafford.

That's what he looks for in every player he signs and he is the same. He never gets tired of winning things. He is a brilliant man.

But that is why I think the hardest decision will be to retire because he is the man who wants success the most.

Sir Alex could go on winning trophies for years and it will be hard for him to give that up."

Steve Bruce

"SIR Alex is absolutely fantastic at getting the right blend of players who want success, who can fit into the dressing room, and who of course have great ability.

They could be the best players in the world but if their attitude was wrong they wouldn't get a look-in at United because they have the potential to upset the dressing room. He always gets the perfect balance.

I think the most important thing he looks for is desire and determination. He wants to know if they have the same desire as him.

That is why United are so successful and why they win trophies every season and why they have carried it on for years.

I think the United squad love success and that is something drummed into them by Sir Alex from the very start."

Gary Neville

"SIR Matt Busby was always seen as the godfather of this club and you would never have thought there would have been another manager like him.

But we have one and he is the manager now. He has surpassed Sir Matt's achievements and in 20, 30 or 40 years time people will look back and see United as formed by two figures, not one."

"The moment of success, of winning a trophy, drains away quickly for me. The euphoria evaporates almost immediately and then I move on. It's just something in me, to create that drug again. You have the excitement at the moment of winning, then you just carry on"

- Sir Alex Ferguson

THE RACE FOR NO.19

Fergie's Men Fully Focused

CRISTIANO RONALDO AND CARLOS TEVEZ MAY BE GONE BUT WITH ANOTHER GROUP OF PROMISING YOUNGSTERS WAITING TO BE UNLEASHED AND A FEW NEW SIGNINGS BOLSTERING THE RANKS, UNITED ARE HUNGRY TO TASTE MORE SUCCESS DURING THE 2009/10 SEASON

WILL 2009/10 be the season which sees United finally knock Liverpool off their perch to become the most successful club in English domestic football?

The late, great Anfield manager Bill Shankly used to describe the championship as Liverpool's bread and butter.

His compatriot, Sir Alex Ferguson, has also seen the league title as the main course on the menu of success he has served up during his Old Trafford dynasty.

And having seen his side edge out Rafael Benitez's men last season to equal Liverpool's record of 18 top-flight crowns, nothing would give Sir Alex more satisfaction than leading United to a 19th triumph.

All eyes will be on the Red Devils as they start life without Cristiano Ronaldo but major stars have left Old Trafford before during Ferguson's reign and he seems to delight in building new teams capable of challenging for silverware.

So while Ronaldo heads up the second wave of Galacticos at the Bernabeu following his world record £80 million transfer, it will be business as usual for United.

With Carlos Tevez having jumped ship to the club's City rivals, there is a certain irony in the fact that if United are to finally overtake Liverpool's number of titles, they will do so relying to some extent on goals from two men who made their name on Merseyside.

It is now almost seven years since Wayne Rooney burst on to the scene in sensational style with Everton and with Ronaldo gone, Sir Alex will be hoping the striker will thrive on the extra responsibility.

Dimitar Berbatov may well prove to be Rooney's regular strike partner but another man with plenty to prove is surprise summer signing Michael Owen.

The former Kop idol seemed to be going stale during a frustrating spell at Newcastle that ended with relegation to the Championship in May.

But Owen does not turn 30 until December and Ferguson snapped him up on a free transfer in a move that will prove increasingly shrewd with every goal he tucks away.

With a World Cup on the horizon at the end of the season, United's new number seven will also be hoping to win over his former Real Madrid boss Fabio Capello.

Owen has only been capped once by England since the Italian took the helm but playing for one of the leading lights in world football – and linking up with Rooney – could see him catapult himself back into the reckoning for a place in the Three Lions' squad for South Africa.

It is well known how much emphasis Owen places on his England career and the carrot of winning a Barclays Premier League medal for the first time could also help him reach another milestone.

He is 10 away from passing United legend Sir Bobby Charlton's record of 49 England goals and will now see a target that once looked like a probability as being a possibility again.

Owen's arrival has not been universally popular among the United support but should he fail to fire, Ferguson has plenty of young talent waiting in the wings.

The 2009/10 campaign could be one which sees Academy graduate Danny Welbeck come to prominence. Sir Alex thinks highly of the Longsight-born striker and has already shown he will have little hesitation in using the England Under-21 front man.

Another teenager who has shown he is happy to take any chance that comes his way is the Italian Federico 'Kiko' Macheda, whose vital intervention as a substitute against Aston Villa last season helped give United

2009/10 PREVIEW

Back in the old routine: United in training during their pre-season trip to Malaysia

FIXTURES 2009/10

AUGUST
16	Birmingham City	H
19	Burnley	A
22	Wigan Athletic	A
29	Arsenal	H

SEPTEMBER
12	Tottenham Hotspur	A
20	Manchester City	H
26	Stoke City	A

OCTOBER
3	Sunderland	H
17	Bolton Wanderers	H
25	Liverpool	A
31	Blackburn Rovers	H

NOVEMBER
8	Chelsea	A
21	Everton	H
28	Portsmouth	A

DECEMBER
5	West Ham United	A
12	Aston Villa	H
15	Wolves	H
19	Fulham	A
26	Hull City	A
28	Wigan Athletic	H

JANUARY
9	Birmingham City	A
16	Burnley	H
26	Hull City	H
30	Arsenal	A

FEBRUARY
6	Portsmouth	H
10	Aston Villa	A
20	Everton	A
27	West Ham United	H

MARCH
6	Wolves	A
13	Fulham	H
20	Liverpool	H
27	Bolton Wanderers	A

APRIL
3	Chelsea	H
10	Blackburn Rovers	A
17	Manchester City	A
24	Tottenham Hotspur	H

MAY
| 1 | Sunderland | A |
| 9 | Stoke City | H |

THE RACE FOR NO.19

some much-needed momentum for the run-in.

Replacing Ronaldo may be an impossible task but Sir Alex has brought in a player who should ensure United continue to pose plenty of threat down the flaks in the shape of Antonio Valencia from Wigan.

The 23-year-old Ecuadorian international signed for a substantial undisclosed fee with Ferguson hoping his pace and ability will help him shine at the Theatre of Dreams.

Another wide player swelling the ranks is Bordeaux's Gabriel Obertan, a man the boss describes as an "exciting prospect".

Aside from the newcomers, Sir Alex has also been keen to reward youngsters who have impressed with new deals.

Midfielder Darron Gibson signed a new three-year contract in July, hot on the heels of goalkeeper Ben Foster who agreed terms on a four-year agreement after Sir Alex hailed him as the successor to Edwin van der Sar.

It may have been a case of smoke and mirrors but upon unveiling Valencia, Owen and Obertan, Sir Alex told journalists there would be no further signings this summer.

"It is the end of our business. Stories about who we are supposed to be getting - forget it," he said.

"It is very difficult to get value now. In a way we benefited through the sale of Cristiano, although that figure was non-negotiable.

"But I feel we have a good squad, which meant there was no need for knee-jerk reactions."

United start the new season at home to newly-promoted Birmingham City with the first crunch clash coming on August 29 when Arsenal are the visitors to Old Trafford.

September sees Mark Hughes bring his new-look Manchester City side to Old Trafford while United visit Anfield for the first of two potentially pivotal fixtures in October.

March and April will see a crucial fortnight with United receiving Liverpool and Chelsea, while the run-in includes trips to Blackburn, the City of Manchester Stadium and Sunderland. The season concludes with the visit of Stoke City and, United will hope, the celebrations following the club's 19th title triumph.

Seventh heaven: Michael Owen will be the successor to Cristiano Ronaldo in the number seven shirt

Leading the line: Dimitar Berbatov is set for a key role this season

MAN UTD SQUAD 2009/10

PLAYER	D.O.B	BIRTHPLACE
Goalkeepers		
Edwin Van der Sar	29.10.70	Voorhout (Hol)
Ben Foster	03.04.83	Leamington Spa
Tomasz Kuszczak	20.03.82	Krosno Odrzaskie (Pol)
Defenders		
Gary Neville	18.02.75	Bury
Patrice Evra	15.05.81	Dakar (Sen)
Rio Ferdinand	07.11.78	Peckham
Wes Brown	13.10.79	Manchester
Nemanja Vidic	21.10.81	Uzice (Ser)
Fabio Da Silva	09.07.90	Petropolis (Bra)
Rafael Da Silva	09.07.90	Petropolis (Bra)
John O'Shea	30.04.81	Waterford
Jonny Evans	02.01.88	Belfast
Danny Simpson	04.01.87	Salford
Midfielders		
Owen Hargreaves	20.01.81	Calgary (Can)
Anderson	13.04.88	Porto Alegre (Bra)
Ryan Giggs	29.11.73	Cardiff
Ji-Sung Park	25.02.81	Seoul (S Kor)
Zoran Tosic	28.04.87	Zrenjanin (Ser)
Michael Carrick	28.07.81	Wallsend
Nani	17.11.86	Praia (Cape Verde)
Paul Scholes	16.11.74	Salford
Darren Fletcher	01.02.84	Edinburgh
Darron Gibson	25.10.87	Derry (ROI)
Rodrigo Possebon	13.02.89	Sapucaia do Sul (Bra)
Antonio Valencia	04.08.85	Nueva Loja (Ecu)
Gabriel Obertan	26.02.89	Pantin (FRa)
Forwards		
Dimitar Berbatov	30.01.81	Blagoevgrad (Bul)
Wayne Rooney	24.10.85	Liverpool
Michael Owen	14.12.79	Chester
Danny Welbeck	26.11.90	Longsight
Federico Macheda	22.08.91	Rome

*UP TO AND INCLUDING 24.07.09